Igniting Worship Series
40 Days with Jesus

Services and Video Clips on DVD

Leith Anderson, Dan Collison, and SpiritFilms™

Abingdon Press
Nashville, Tennessee

IGNITING WORSHIP SERIES: 40 DAYS WITH JESUS

This book is printed on acid-free, recycled paper.

Library of Congress Cataloging-in-Publication Data

Anderson, Leith, 1944–
   40 days with Jesus : services and video clips on DVD / Leith Anderson, Dan Colllison.
      p.   cm. — (Igniting worship series)
   ISBN 0-687-33351-2
1. Lent.   2. Worship programs.   3. Jesus Christ—Passion.   I. Title: Forty days with Jesus.   II.Collison, Dan.   III. Title.   IV. Series.

BV85.A53   2006
264—dc22

2006000101

ISBN-13: 978-0-687-33351-6

07 08 09 10 11 12 13 14 15—10 9 8 7 6 5 4 3 2

MANUFACTURED IN THE UNITED STATES OF AMERICA

Contents

Introduction: A Glimpse of God's Glory

Each week the pastors, staff, and volunteers of Wooddale Church seek to give worshipers a glimpse of God's glory through meaningful and prayerfully planned worship events. These experiences must be appropriate for those who believe and also for those who do not yet know God. They must relate biblical truth to everyday life. They must be inspiring, uplifting, and encouraging. They must always be open to the leading and influence of the Holy Spirit. Yet they must realistically occur within a set time frame. Ministering through worship requires careful thought, constant prayer, and dedication to excellence. It's hard work.

Our desire is that this resource will provide structure and insight as you also conceive, plan, and implement powerful worship at your church. We will share resources to support what you are currently doing and perhaps provide insight as you pursue new challenges. It is our hope that you will find the direction you need to implement new elements of worship (drama, faith stories, etc.) and add dimension to worship at your church.

The apostle John saw a vision of "a great multitude that no one could count, from every nation, tribe, people and language, standing before the throne and in front of the Lamb" (Revelation 7:9). This picture of the church at worship provides a startling, celebratory picture of what we will someday experience together. It inspires us to the constant, creative pursuit of excellence and to deeper expressions of worship of our great God.

I. THE STARTING POINT

Why should we worship God? What is worship? Does the style of worship matter to God? Should we plan worship? What do we want to happen to people in the worship experience? People that design worship a minimum of fifty-two times a year do not have time to ruminate on these questions, but their answers and attitudes about them will nonetheless be reflected in the worship events they plan. Perfect answers are out of our reach, at least during this life; however, we should thoughtfully consider the questions.

Why should we worship God?

We are created to worship God. It is essential for our existence and vital for our spiritual survival. Worship reaches to the core purpose of our intricate design, and to not worship would be like owning a car you never drive or a house you never live in. Cars are manufactured to be driven, houses are created to be lived in, and we are designed to worship God (Exodus 19:6; 1 Peter 2:9).

What is worship?

To this question, some people might respond, "Worship is meeting at the church building to sing songs and listen to a sermon." Others might say, "Worship is a specific order of liturgy." These brief definitions describe specific actions that encourage people to worship, but they do not define worship itself. At Wooddale Church we believe that: "Worship is an explicit invitation to experience the divine mystery of God's manifest presence in life transforming ways." The Bible clearly teaches that God is omnipresent. Yet, it is also evident throughout the Bible that in the midst of worship experiences something wonderful (even overwhelming!) occurred: God made himself especially present, or manifest. To this end, we have framed a working worship theology statement as follows:

Wooddale Church Theology of Worship

In life

Worship is above all a lifestyle of acknowledging God in every facet of our lives. The Bible makes it clear that God delights in our worship of him. In fact, according to Jesus, worshiping God is so much a part of who we were created to be that if we don't worship him, the rocks will cry out (Luke 19:40)! Further, God wants us to worship him sincerely with our whole being, in spirit and truth (John 4:23–24).

In community

Worship is a gift from God and not a human invention. It is an explicit invitation to experience the divine mystery of God's manifest presence in life transforming ways. This occurs on both personal and corporate levels; however, there is a marked spiritual potency in larger gatherings of people. The Bible demonstrates that, as the people of God gather in community to worship, there are tangible results of personal transformation and empowerment for the purpose of advancing the Kingdom of God. From the Exodus event to New Testament church meetings, the presence of God was made manifest when people worshiped together.

As a witness

We believe that worship is one of the most effective outreach tools available to the church today. What other Christian context offers seekers the opportunity to experience authentic prayer, meaningful life stories, relevant biblical teaching, stirring music and interaction with others seeking God? We strive to design worship as a safe place for both Christians and pre-Christians to experience God.

Does the style of worship matter to God?

Style certainly matters to people! Take an informal survey about what people like best in their worship services, and most likely you'll hear passionate responses like: "Contemporary music is the only way I can feel God," or, "Traditional worship moves me deeply." Are these comments wrong? Well, it would be refreshing to hear, "I just love God and it doesn't matter really what style of service I attend." Reality, however, dictates that we connect people to God from where they are—including where they are in their stylistic preferences.

This is not a new idea. Throughout biblical history, the styles and forms of worship continually changed. Some transformations were initiated by God and others simply by the imposition of practical necessity. Two examples in the Old Testament are Moses in the Exodus event and King David in the reforming of the Israeli national identity. Mosaic worship reflects a highly patterned and institutional form of worship based upon sacrifice and offerings, yet it had very little music. King David shaped worship with a great deal of music and included non-sacrificial practices. Both worship identities were designed to draw people to God in new ways appropriate to societal changes and conditions.

So, we now ask: "Is the focus of this worship style upon God?" If our ever-changing styles are focused on God, then yes, style matters to God; however, only insomuch as it directs everyone to God. Reflecting this, Wooddale Church has established a philosophy of worship:

Wooddale Church Philosophy of Worship

Audience of One

Wooddale Church approaches worship much the way Christian philosopher Søren Kierkegaard did. He believed that in worship we have an audience of One. Those in the congregation are the performers; the leaders on the platform are the coaches; and God is the audience.

Stylistic approach

The chosen styles of worship at Wooddale Church are traditional and contemporary. Equal attention and value are placed on both styles to provide excellence and diversity for Christians and pre-Christians of all ages and demographics. We further define our stylistic approaches in a worship purpose statement:

The purpose of Wooddale Church's worship services is to honor God by providing weekly services that:

- Engage believers in an authentic traditional worship experience utilizing classical music, traditional forms and liturgies, in culturally relevant forms and . . .

- Engage believers in an authentic contemporary worship experience utilizing contemporary, culturally relevant forms and...

In both styles:

- Engage seekers in varied stylistic experiences that provide them an opportunity to interact with believers and to consider the truths of Christianity for their own lives.

Cultural relevance

Since the beginning of human history people have worshiped using the communication methods and art forms of their particular culture and time. Likewise, we want to worship God in biblical, meaningful and relevant 21st-Century cultural forms.

Should we plan worship?

We plan weddings, family reunions, birthday parties, and business deals. The success or failure of these events usually lies in how well the event was planned. Worship is no different—except that what we are planning is a God event! Out of a passion for God and a desire to connect people to God, planning worship should be one of the highest priorities of every church.

What do we want to happen to people in the worship experience?

We want people to experience God. Several wonderful things can happen. People can: begin or renew a relationship with Jesus Christ, make a deeper commitment of some part of their life to God, receive emotional or physical healing, gain life perspective, obtain a greater understanding of the world around them, learn biblical truth, learn to love others, and—most important—become more like Jesus Christ.

II. WORSHIP CONCEPTION: CREATIVE BEGINNINGS

Peering through the lenses of our worship theology and philosophy, the Celebration Arts Leadership Team (music, drama, media, senior pastor, and visual arts) begins the planning process by taking two important steps:

- Gather all critical planning information

- Engage the creative planning system

Gather critical information

We live in an age of vast information. We have more worship topics for discussion and development than can possibly be addressed—even with fifty-two weekends of worship experiences to plan. The first challenge of worship planning teams is to discern which concepts to focus upon. It makes sense to assemble critical information from three gathering points: the culture around us, our congregational life, and the leadership of the church.

Gathering point #1: The culture around us

Wooddale Church views culture as a sociological realization of the patterned ways that people live their lives. Therefore, paying keen attention to how our culture is developing, we can create accessible modes and means of delivery for worship (i.e. learning styles, visual connections, artistic meanings, and communication media). Asking questions can aid the process:

- What in our culture is viewing God in a positive way?

- What is acting against God that may need a response?

- What events are on the minds of people coming to worship?

- What overarching thoughts and emotions are being experienced in our times?

Gathering point #2: Congregational life

This gathering point centers on issues and questions that are raised from within our congregation. Frequently, the Celebration Arts Leadership Team collects information from the congregation through formal and informal surveys in the worship services, conversations in the hallways, feedback that is given to pastors and staff, and general assessments of the congregational life at Wooddale Church. We focus on strategically gathering information related to a topic just before the particular sermon or sermon series.

Gathering point #3: Church leadership

One of the primary roles of the church leadership is to ensure that the congregation is being taught the entire counsel of God's Word. Attention is given to prioritizing specific topics and issues so as to provide a balanced approach to attaining discipleship in the Christian life.

Leadership training for pastors includes quarterly retreat days where there are intentional experiences with some aspect of the regional culture. These retreat days are spent visiting educational institutions, cultural attractions, area churches and denominations, religious centers, and other points of interest. The elders and pastors have an annual planning day in which they decide upon the overall church objectives and strategies for the following year. All of these leadership formation events lead to the choice of thematic content for Wooddale Church's worship experiences.

Engage the creative planning system

Having good information is important, but what do we do with all of the gathered information and directives? We pour it into a *creative planning system—an agreed upon schedule of meetings and objectives that shapes the worship experience from beginning to end.*

Building a system of creative design is one of the most important functional jobs that worship leaders can provide for their team(s) of creative people. Not having a system for worship design contributes to anxiety and ministry burnout.

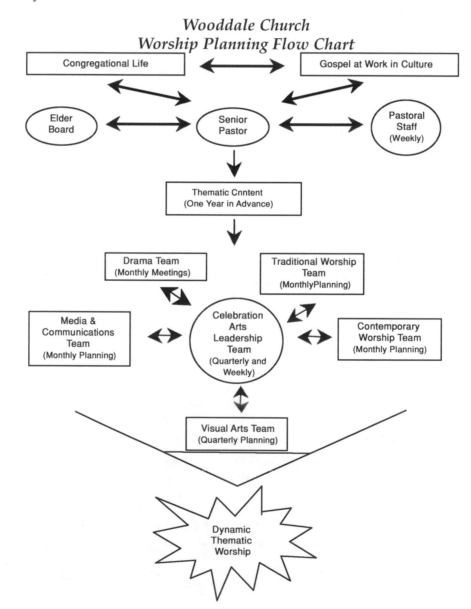

Wooddale Church
Worship Planning Flow Chart

- *Quarterly Celebration Arts meetings* are held to discuss service content *six months ahead.* These are the "big picture, dreams, and visions" meetings. People present: senior pastor, executive pastor of program, celebration arts pastor, events manager, music, drama, media, children's choir leaders, and an administrative assistant.

- *Monthly worship team meetings* focus on the specific style and service types forming the details of each service *six to eight weeks ahead.* This includes the traditional leadership team, contemporary leadership team, drama, and media.

- *Weekly pastoral staff meetings.* This meeting occurs first thing on Monday mornings and covers a repeating agenda as well as any current projects requiring pastoral staff efforts. One of the agenda items is to evaluate the worship experience from the past weekend.

- *Weekly Celebration Arts Leadership Team meetings* on Wednesday afternoons are designed to evaluate past worship experiences and plan the details for future experiences. The greatest focus of this weekly meeting is on the upcoming weekend.

Some church leaders reading this might say: "There is no way that we could be that organized. We are simply not administratively minded." However, even non-administrative people can thrive in a system if they build a team of people that will agree to work together on a schedule of meetings and deadlines. Taking the time upfront to set meetings will guarantee that, at the very least, you will be thinking ahead!

III. THE POWER OF THEME IN WORSHIP

Advertising copywriters, politicians, and pastors have many differences, but they do share one conviction—a common belief in the power of theme. Without a clear and focused theme, communication is impossible. One observer said, "What is fog in the pulpit becomes a mist in the pews." In creating powerful, relevant and memorable worship experiences it is imperative to begin with a clear sense of what we want people to take away, believe, or do. With a clear theme, all those involved in creating the experience can select elements—music, drama, visuals, and faith story (each explained in the pages that follow)—that reinforce the central guiding idea of the experience. Without a theme, worshipers encounter a series of unrelated elements that lack coherence and may, in fact, distract from the message.

Series

What *theme* creates for a worship service, a series can provide over a period of time. Most people like a certain amount of continuity. A theme developed over several weeks can create a sense of anticipation. Grouping a series of themes can provide an overarching context for individual messages. Too much continuity can become boring, but each new series allows for variety—not only of theme, but also of communication approach and creative elements. Drama, visuals, prayer, and other tools can be utilized in unique ways over a condensed time frame, offering both freshness and continuity. Naming a series in an interesting and creative way can reinforce communication and signal the key ideas. In doing so, it is important to strike a balance between rewarding those who participate throughout the series and making each week accessible to those who've just dropped in. One challenge is finding a series name when moving through a Bible book. It is often easier to name a topical series, but identifying a key theme in a book can give people a way to understand individual messages in the context of the whole book.

Examples:

Biblical

- **Biography of Jesus**—Luke

- **Peter's Principles**—1 Peter

- **Famous Bible Stories**—Old Testament highlights

- **Four Christmas Gospels**—Matthew 1:18–25, Mark 1:1–13, Luke 2:1–20, John 1:1–18

Topical

- **Becoming Jesus' Disciple**—Bible, faith, prayer, church, serving, giving, sharing

- **Loving**—Love, loving God, loving self, loving one another, loving my neighbor, loving my enemy, loving your marriage partner

- **Sermons People Want to Hear**—Near death experiences, good living, relationships, angels, end times

- **What We Want in Life**—Love, hope, peace, forgiveness, pleasure, meaning, eternal life

- **Christian View of . . .**—Islam, fear, morality, busyness, talents

- **Healthy Attitudes**—Suffering, conflict, money, relationships, work, change, parents & parenting, uncertainty

- **Bible Animals**—Snake (temptation and sin); scapegoat (forgiveness); ravens (special to God); ant (work); lion (ultimate victory of Jesus)

- **Outreach 21**—Twenty-one ways to reach out (three week series)

- **Divine Healing**—God's grace, relationships, physical healing

Special Occasions

- **Christmas Choices**—Mary (faith); Joseph (righteousness); Shepherds (coming to Jesus); Magi (going great distances to Jesus)

- **Easter Eyewitnesses**—Jewish officials (belief in Jesus); Barabbas (substitution); John (loyalty to Jesus); Thomas (doubting and believing)

Title

A good title can help draw in the listener, summarize the big idea, and relate well to real life. Titles can be unimaginatively simple, a mere summarization of the theme, or an intriguing description of the text.

Instead of:

"Repentance," try "When All Else Fails, What About Plan B"
"Work Hard," try "Work Like an Ant"
"Moses and the Burning Bush," try "When God Interrupts"
"Jesus Calms the Storm," try "Can Jesus Be Trusted?"
"The Rich Young Ruler," try "The Guy Who Had Everything and Still Wasn't Satisfied"

Catchy titles are not always the best method. Care should be taken when using movie titles and colloquial expressions, especially when force-fit. These can work if used sparingly and before the expression becomes trite or overused. Contemporary culture often has a short shelf life.

The best titles clearly communicate the theme. Better to be clear and dull, than clever and confusing. Good titles are full of hope. A gloom and doom title often turns off interest rather than brings people in. It is also important to connect the title to real life. "Give your worries to God" connects to everyone and does so more positively than "Don't worry."

When titling a sermon, think of who might be attending. Using insider language ("Be a Barnabas") or confrontational tone ("Steal no longer") immediately creates barriers with unbelievers. Instead, use positive language that is familiar to all ("Be an encourager").

Theme

Theme is the unifying subject or idea around which all the elements of a worship experience revolve. This could be a theological concept (grace, creation, providence, sin, etc.), a biblical virtue (honesty, contentment, compassion, obedience, etc.), a biblical theme (love, faithfulness, blessings, justice, etc.) or a topical issue (war, poverty, sexuality, etc.). Most important is defining the theme clearly and succinctly so that it gives all those involved in creating the worship experience the guidance they need to work the theme into all elements.

Sermon summary

It's great to have a sermon idea in mind, but unless the idea is clearly captured on paper, those around you will never know where it is going. A sermon summary briefly outlines the key idea to be communicated. It articulates the main point of the sermon so that those working on music, drama, visuals, and other service elements can easily know how to integrate the theme into their planning. For example:

Title: "Scapegoat—Getting Away with Sin"
Series: Bible Animals #2
Text: Leviticus 16:8, 10, 26
Theme: Forgiveness of sin
Summary: One of the strangest and most wonderful animals in the Bible was the scapegoat. Unlike other animals that were sacrificed to atone for human sins, the scapegoat took the sins and ran for the wilderness. Imagine the feelings of those ancient people who saw their sins passed to an animal who got to live but ran far away.
Specials: Post-it® notes in program to write sins on.

The sticky factor

The most interesting and spirited conversations of the entire creative planning process occur around the sticky factor. The sticky factor is exactly as it sounds—taking the chosen thematic content and making it as sticky as possible so as to grab the worshipers' attention and adhere to them as they leave the worship experience. Some creative planners have called this *the use of metaphor*. Essentially, it involves finding a root image or object to connect the worshiper with the ideas being presented in worship. Obvious choices are movie clips and live dramatic illustrations. Some more "out of the box" creative examples that we have used include:

• A live goat was used to illustrate the Old Testament concept of the "scapegoat and sending sin away." Post-it® notes were placed in every worship program. At a select point in the service those participating in the worship experience were asked to write down on the note a sin they wanted to get rid of. The notes were then collected and placed in a bag, which was then placed on a live (trained!) goat on the platform. The goat was led out of the worship space, and a pre-produced video was shown of the goat leaving the campus.

- Two Ford Thunderbird cars were used to express the theme of "being special to God." One brand new Thunderbird and one collector's Thunderbird—corresponding to the years that they were named the "car of the year"—were placed at the two main church entrances to give people a visual metaphor for "being special." These cars became a conversation point for individuals in their work environments and gave worshipers an opportunity to share their faith.

- An electric chainsaw was used to enhance a sermon about how harsh words are like careless chainsaw work. Both can do regrettable damage.

IV. WORSHIP SERVICE DESIGN: PUTTING IT ALL TOGETHER

The theology and philosophy behind the worship service have been established. Broad research has been done. Thematic content has been chosen. Now it is time to put all the pieces of worship together into one cohesive experience.

1. Gather all of the planned elements of worship.

This includes the preaching calendar with broad assignments, the worship planning templates with the specific assignments, drama scripts, faith story schedule, and musical resources from the leadership teams.

2. Plan the essential details first.

This includes writing a technical script for each worship time. Worship orders must take into consideration where the speaker, the faith story presenter, and the drama actors need to be during concurrent services as well as all scheduled periodic events like communion and baptism.

3. Create a dynamic worship experience!

The greatest task of the music/worship pastor is to navigate the necessary timing and details while still accomplishing several things:

- Create a seamless and dynamic experience with transitions between elements

- Shape the emotional flow of the experience so as to not overwhelm or underwhelm the worshiper

- Provide the worshiper an opportunity to prepare, receive, and respond to God's Word through the various elements of the experience

These three steps coordinate all aspects of the worship experience: sermon, music, media, drama, faith story, periodic elements, and visual arts.

A. The Sermon

Preaching in the last century has often confronted and condemned. Perhaps past generations responded well to negative messages, but the same is not true today. People come into our churches feeling discouraged, depressed, tired, lonely, and guilty. They are more interested in what to do about their sins and struggles than about being reminded of what they are. Most people get beat up six days a week and come to church to find hope. They want "good news"—news that God loves them and wants to see them live life to the full. This doesn't mean that we don't address sin or take up prophetic themes but that when we do, we point people to answers and hope in God.

In addition to hope, people come to hear how the truth of the Bible relates to everyday life. We need to connect to contemporary events and culture, but we must do so through the lens of timeless biblical truth. That means being both faithful to the text and able to relate it to contemporary life.

B. Music

Music is the glue of the worship experience. It connects the elements of worship and—at the same time—intimately connects the worshiper to God through prayer, poetry, and theological reflection delivered in a variety of styles. In the Wooddale Church worship experiences, we utilize both traditional and contemporary music styles. People frequently ask Pastor Leith Anderson, "Which musical style do you prefer?" He replies, "That is like asking me which of my children I prefer. I love both." At Wooddale Church, we assume a sibling approach (equal time and attention) to our music styles. We promote teamwork and avoid rivalry. On the chart at the top of the next page, you will see some other important distinctions.

Content	Traditional Worship	Contemporary Worship
Sermon, faith story, drama	Same	Same
Music style(s)	Classical	Jazz and rock
Attire (Preacher changes clothes between services)	Business	Business casual to casual formal
Musicians	Choir and organ featured; classical instruments augment, including symphonic percussion as needed	Vocalists on microphones, electronic instruments, and standard rhythm section
Types of songs	Hymns and a few choruses	Choruses and a few hymns re-arranged for contemporary band setting
Frequency of repeating songs	Long shelf life for hymns, thus infrequent usage of a large amount of songs	Short shelf life for choruses, thus a "radio play" type of approach following popularity and desirability
Media	Limited use of media. PowerPoint for sermons, more static backgrounds and graphics	Video intensive with some moving background images
Creeds and historical prayers	Frequent rotation of items like the Apostle's Creed and the Lord's Prayer	Infrequent (approx 1–2 times a year) usage
Communion	Same, but with classical instrumental music	Same, but with reflective instrumental and vocal music.
Prayer	Usually incorporates an invocation and some responsively read prayers	Informal, usually added to existing elements like songs, sermon or announcements

What about blended worship?

Many churches across America have "blended" worship services. Often, this is the best use of resources and personnel. In our larger church setting, we have found that providing the option of two choices keeps both styles of worship keyed in on what specific music and setting draws people to God. From time to time at Wooddale Church, we combine the styles to have blended worship for special events.

Putting music in the worship experience

Block plan several services
Grouping as few as two and as many as eight services into one planning day enables the designer to look over several weeks at once to craft song usage and music personnel and to keep ahead of the preparation that is needed on a week to week basis.

Gather all of the song suggestions
It's best to have multiple lists of music available during the planning process. These lists may include:

- A master list organized in an Excel document with song title, key, copyright info, and music.

- A short list of new and recent songs ready for rotation.

- Worship software that helps search the larger list of available songs beyond what is in the current music library.

Read the Bible passages for each week and think about various approaches to the theme
For example the theme might be "prayer," but what kind of prayer? Confession? Intercession? Persistent?

Choose congregational songs based upon several criteria:

- Does the song make sense theologically?

- Is it memorable and easy to learn?

- Is it able to draw people into worship?

- Can the congregation sing it?

Customize the music
Thinking about new ways to deliver the music ensures that the worship event always feels fresh. This may mean rearranging an existing song or using a different instrumentation or vocal construction. The worship experiences can feel "custom" even if many of the elements are similar or have been used before.

Sequence the music
Creating flow and sequence in the music is essential for establishing an effective emotional experience. Great worship is like telling a story that has an introduction, development of the theme, a climax, and a final conclusion. Some important considerations include musical or spoken transitions between songs, key changes to lead into more songs, tempo selection, and instrumental bridges between songs.

Monitor the frequency of songs
All songs have a shelf life, and each congregation has different processing spans for the music they sing.

Traditional—Hymns need to be rotated on a much less frequent basis than choruses to avoid overusage.

Contemporary—When introducing a song into contemporary worship, it should be sung two to three times within the first few months that it is learned. After the initial introduction, allow four to six weeks before reusing the same song.

Incorporate instrumentals
Instrumentals can be used in preludes and postludes or during a time of reflection. Consider using unique music that contributes to the service, heightens the worship experience, provides a meaningful background to prayer, or inspires a deeper level of involvement in the service.

C. Media

Planning media elements in worship requires a great degree of coordination because media is directly tied to what is happening live in the room. The media team must be informed about the various elements of the worship experience, including:

Theme of the service

What group of images will connect the worshiper to the meaning of the sermon? What songs will relate to the theme as a whole?

Seasonal and stylistic visual concepts

What color palettes, patterns, and images are acceptable to use for visual images?

Music concepts and feel

What screen backgrounds, wording, and lighting reflect both the theological content and the emotional mood of the individual songs and teachings?

Video synchronization

Can moving video be used effectively to enhance live music, drama, or speaking?

D. Drama

The drama ministry at Wooddale Church seeks to effectively convey God's truths through the theatrical arts and expand the worship experience by using the God-given gifts of drama team members. Dramas make human circumstances and stories come alive. They are a powerful way to communicate with worshipers.

The drama ministry is . . .

- diverse in style and venue

- a creative way to help worshipers apply God's truths to their own lives and consider issues of faith in a fresh way

- another way to expand and encourage worship

- a creative discipline that brings glory to God

- a way of underscoring or illuminating the service's theme and scripture

The drama ministry is not . . .

- preaching, sermonizing, or pat answers

- entertainment or performance in and of itself

- a showcase for the talents of participants

- a way for participants to deliver their own messages on general religious thought

The ideal drama ministry

A thriving drama ministry can be simple or expansive. It can focus primarily on dramas to introduce the sermon (or conclude it), or it can include weekly, age-appropriate, children's ministry dramas. It can include outreach events (dinner theaters, musicals, reviews). It can incorporate religious and non-religious material. Above all, it should provide opportunities for artists—whether established or emerging—to use their God-given gifts to glorify God. *"If you speak, you should do so as one who speaks the very words of God. If you serve, you should do so with the strength God provides, so that in all things God may be praised through Jesus Christ. To him be the glory and the power for ever and ever. Amen."* (Peter 4:11)

E. FaithStory

A faith story is a five-minute presentation by individuals sharing how they came to believe in Jesus Christ or how they are sharing their faith in Jesus Christ with others. These stories are deliberately connected with the worship theme. They powerfully reinforce the message.

The purpose of a faith story is to:

- Explain the process of coming to believe in Jesus Christ through personal commitment to him

- Affirm the purpose and values of Wooddale Church

- Provide a real life example of the truth communicated through the service's message and music

- Challenge unbelievers to consider Christian faith

- Encourage believers

At Wooddale Church, the discipleship pastor manages the faith story program. After reviewing the preaching schedule and understanding the themes for specific worship services, the recruitment begins. Presenters are typically found through the church membership process or various programs and referrals from staff.

Presenters are recruited months in advance, given a set of written guidelines, and coached through the development of their presentation. When the first draft of the story is written, presenters submit it to the discipleship pastor for review and editing. A personal, face-to-face meeting (normally 30–45 minutes) takes place, with suggestions given to strengthen the story. The discipleship pastor helps the speaker to present his or her story clearly. The pastor edits words and concepts that can be confusing or offensive. Typically, the presenter writes three drafts before the final version is fully prepared.

F. Periodic Elements

There are several periodic elements that cycle through the worship experiences at Wooddale Church, and the treatment of each item can provide extraordinary moments of transformation during worship.

Communion

Communion is celebrated on the first weekend of each month. Before the elements are passed, the pastor gives a clear presentation of the gospel and offers participants an opportunity to begin a relationship with Jesus Christ. The music during communion is always reflective and draws the worshiper into a greater focus upon God and commitment to him. The features of worship leading up to and immediately following communion provide emotional and thematic "pivots" to integrate the communion experience into the service as a whole.

Baptism

Individuals being baptized are asked to prepare and share a very brief story of their faith journey. This is a powerful demonstration of their faith in Jesus and his power at work in their lives. Baptisms are a celebration shared between the individual, the pastor, the worshipers and God.

Special prayer

Prayer and worship can be seamless because both are communication with God. Directed prayer with music, dedication prayers for individuals and written or historical prayers are all effective in adding a spoken texture to the worship experience.

G Visual Arts

The visual arts ministry is still in an emergent phase at Wooddale Church and takes place mostly outside of the worship space but in highly visible areas of the church building. The visual arts coordinate all visual artistic activity with the thematic worship design of the church as a whole. Thus, the visual arts enhance the worship experience by drawing people into the following worship themes:

- Christmas

- Easter

- Art show following a worship service theme for the summer

- Art show following a worship service theme for the fall

- Art show with a general winter theme (i.e. "Quilting as Art")

- Art show to engage younger artists (i.e., "Young at Art" for kindergarten through high school age artists)

Visual Arts Purpose Statement

The purpose of the visual arts ministry team is to honor God in the disciple-making process by using the visual arts to enrich the worship experience, by helping the Wooddale Church congregation identify and develop God-given creative abilities through educational opportunities, and by encouraging the stewardship of artistic skills.

This ministry seeks to provide avenues for the Wooddale Church community (1) to use the visual arts to respond to God in worship and praise and (2) to reach out to our community by using the visual arts as a medium.

Ministry goals are:

- Regarding worship, to explore and encourage ways of using the visual arts in worship

- Regarding stewardship, to encourage visual artists to develop and use their skills to enhance the life of the church

- Regarding education, to provide art activities and events for children and adults

- Regarding community, to provide a connection point and growth opportunity for people with an interest and/or ability in the visual arts

V. THE FINAL STEP: IMPLEMENTATION AND EVALUATION

Worship and Excellence

"Whatever you do, work at it with all your heart, as working for the Lord, not for human masters . . . It is the Lord Christ you are serving." (Colossians 3:23–24)

An overarching passion of the Celebration Arts ministry at Wooddale Church is to glorify God or—as we like to say—"make God look good." This is accomplished by having teams of people serve in the implementation and evaluation of the worship experience.

Implementing and Executing the Worship Plan

Implementing the worship plan is the follow-through, or execution, of all the previous week's planning. This is the schedule of the process we follow:

Monday:
- Weekly pastoral staff meeting includes a time of debriefing the past weekend's services; a review of all worship service items for the coming weekend, including possible changes to the order, listing of worship announcements, special elements, detail, and key timing issues

- Celebration Arts staff finalizes the service orders and distributes the content to publications, ushers, worship leaders, custodial staff, and music teams

Tuesday:
- Contemporary music is prepared and rehearsed in the evening. Vocals rehearse alone from 6:15–7:00 PM. The entire contemporary worship team meets for a devotion and small group prayer from 7:00–7:30 PM and then rehearses from 7:30–9:00 PM

- The media team completes visuals for the contemporary worship experience, sets up for rehearsal, and participates in the rehearsal

Wednesday:
- The worship program is sent to the printer

- Celebration Arts Leadership Team meets and goes through the elements of each service in full detail

- Traditional worship music is prepared along with choir news and all details for the evening rehearsal. Instrumentalists rehearse from 6:30–7:00 PM and the choir then joins from 7:00–8:15 PM. Devotion and prayer take place at the end of rehearsal.

Thursday and Friday:
- Finalization of all media elements including sermon PowerPoint presentation

- Drama team rehearses production for weekend services

Saturday:
- Rehearsal for Saturday services, including set-up and 45 minute rehearsal of contemporary worship team

- Drama sound check and rehearsal (if needed)

- 5:15 PM worship service

- Video tape the sermon for Sunday AM backup purposes

- Review all timing elements of the worship service and make adjustments for Sunday

Sunday:
- Early meeting of all key worship leaders for prayer and final details

- Synchronization of all clocks to ensure effective concurrent worship service schedule accuracy

- Sound check of all music teams in all worship spaces

- Sound check for drama team

- Five worship services in two worship spaces: 9:00 AM contemporary and traditional, 10:15 AM contemporary and traditional, 11:30 AM contemporary

Contingency planning for the unexpected

Two questions leaders regularly ask are, "What if it doesn't work?" and, "What if it really works?" Murphy's Law bluntly suggests that sometime, somewhere, something will go wrong. What if there is a power outage or a storm on Sunday morning? What if there's a medical emergency in the front row of the auditorium? What if the pastor becomes ill and can't preach? What if a person with mental illness decides to come up on stage with a word from God? Suppose an Easter marketing blitz brings in 50 percent more people than you expected? Or the grand opening of your new facility brings hundreds more than expected? What will you do?

Rather than live with the anxiety of what might go wrong, you can anticipate and develop contingency plans that will give you the confidence needed to respond to unlikely but possible circumstances. Imagine various scenarios. Write down logical steps and responsible parties. In general, the simpler the plan, the more likely it will be both remembered and implemented. It's important to always define the decision-maker and to keep any written plans in a place where they can be readily accessed.

One way Wooddale Church has chosen to plan for unexpected issues during a service is to designate an additional pastor/elder to be "pastor in service." This individual sits in the first or second row and serves as a point person for whoever is leading the service and preaching. In the case of an emergency, this individual is ready to take direction from the pastor on the platform or to take action if necessary.

Evaluation

It takes courage to evaluate your own work. Yet, evaluation can be a healthy, affirming, and enriching experience—the key to growing and addressing new challenges.

Evaluate regularly

Twice weekly we examine the worship experience—on Mondays at pastoral staff meetings and on Wednesdays during Celebration Arts team meetings. Discussions include reviews of the specifics from the previous week as well as issues that have broader impact on the overall worship planning system (e.g., how information is delivered, weekly practices, and delivery modes).

Evaluate in a positive manner

Respect, concern, and patience are marks of good evaluation meetings. Problem solving is rarely a fun activity, but when everyone at the evaluation table communicates in a manner that is encouraging, non-defensive, and informative, most people are willing to bring about the necessary changes so that excellence can grow.

Evaluate by asking the big questions

Was it challenging, compelling, and encouraging? Did it connect biblical truth to life? Was it presented with excellence that honors God, inspires believers, and attracts seekers?

Service 1

Greatness in Humility

THEME

Humility

BIBLE PASSAGES

John 1:1–5, 14
In the beginning was the Word, and the Word was with God, and the Word was God. He was with God in the beginning. Through him all things were made; without him nothing was made that has been made. In him was life, and that life was the light of all people. The light shines in the darkness, and the darkness has not overcome it. The Word became flesh and made his dwelling among us.

Philippians 2:5–11
In your relationships with one another, have the same attitude of mind Christ Jesus had: Who, being in very nature God, did not consider equality with God something to be used to his own advantage; rather, he made himself nothing by taking the very nature of a servant, being made in human likeness. And being found in appearance as a human being, he humbled himself by becoming obedient to death—even death on a cross. Therefore God exalted him to the highest place and gave him the name that is above every name, that at the name of Jesus every knee should bow, in heaven and on earth and under the earth, and every tongue acknowledge that Jesus Christ is Lord, to the glory of God the Father.

SUMMARY

The eternal, invisible Son of God stepped down from all the power and glory of heaven to become human. He was conceived in a mortal body, lived a fully human life, endured ridicule, and suffered torture and death. In all this, he was not lowered but elevated. In his astonishing humility, he demonstrated true greatness. Now Jesus calls us to walk in humility following his example.

SERVICE IMAGE

The DVD features a graphic image suitable for use during the "Greatness in Humility" service. This suggested worship background is a photograph of a person's hands pouring water from a pitcher into a basin. This worship background appears on the *Abingdon Worship Photos, vol 3: Projection Images for Lent and Easter,* by Jim and Mary Whitmer (2003, Abingdon).

CONTEMPORARY SERVICE SEQUENCE:

Prelude

"Creator King" by Mary MacLean (© 2003 Vertical Worship Songs c/o Integrity Media Inc.)

> Key Lyrics: "Who am I that you are mindful of me . . . who am I that you set your love upon me . . . you're my creator King"

> Resources: Listening CD—*Satisfy,* by Kathryn Scott (2003, Vertical Worship). Video—iWORSHIP DVD, vol H, at www.integritymusic.com. Printed music at www.praisecharts.com.

This song leads worshipers into the theme of humility by reflecting upon their position in the universe and with God. This song can be used in a number of ways: as a solo or with a group, with instruments or with tracks, and with lyrics projected over the video image or without.

Worship Through Music

The flow of these three songs in the opening singing is summed up in a prayer (that could be used somewhere during the songs): *"Lord Jesus, King of creation, please come to us and our wandering hearts. Focus our hearts and minds upon you. Humbly, we ask for your daily provision as we sing aloud that we are hungry for your presence in our lives, our church, and our world."*

"Come Thou Fount of Every Blessing" words by Robinson, music by John Wyeth (Public domain)
> Key Lyrics: "Tune my heart to sing your grace"

"The Lord's Prayer" by Matt Shepardson (© 1999 Ever Devoted Music)
> Key Lyrics: "Father in heaven . . . all praise be to your name…Your kingdom come, your will be done on earth as it is in heaven" (This is a modern, upbeat arrangement of the Lord's Prayer.)

> Resource: Lyrics, video, demo track, rehearsal track, and printed music at www.willowcreek.com/resources/music.asp (Search for "The Lord's Prayer" or use the following url—http://www.willowcreek.com/arrangement.asp?action=details&arrangementid=1140&sid=12)

"We Are Hungry" by Brad Kilman (© 1999 Brad Kilman Publishing/ASCAP)

> Key Lyrics: "We are hungry, we are thirsty for more of you"

Resource: Listening CD—*Clouds are Forming*, by Brad Kilman (available at www.grassrootsmusic.com). Listening CD—*The Road to One Day*, by Passion Conferences (2000, Sparrow/Emd). Listening CD—*Window to the Inner Court*, by Shane Everett (2001, available at www.grassrootsmusic.com)

Welcome

During the welcome, the pastor greets all participants in the worship service and invites them to connect to the worship series, "40 Days with Jesus," by participating in church-wide small groups, education, and serving opportunities that launch this week's emphasis on humility.

Worship Through Teaching

GREATNESS IN HUMILITY
John 1:1–5, 14; Philippians 2:5–11

I want to talk to you about Jesus. Not about religion or churches or denominations. Not about controversial doctrines or historic institutions: just Jesus. Because when we experience Jesus, when we meet him and get to know him, all these other things become less important.

For someone who is so famous, it is surprising that we know nothing about his physical appearance. You would think that at least one of his biographers would have described his height and weight, the color of his hair and his eyes, or the shade of his skin. Is it that they didn't notice or that they considered it unimportant? Or did they become so enthralled with the man that his appearance didn't matter?

His story starts before the beginning. Whether you calculate the beginning of time to be 4000 BCE or 4000 billion trillion BCE, he was there before the beginning. He is more ancient than time itself. Here's the way his best friend and biographer John describes him in John 1:1–5:

> *In the beginning was the Word, and the Word was with God, and the Word was God. He was with God in the beginning. Through him all things were made; without him nothing was made that has been made. In him was life, and that life was the light of all people. The light shines in the darkness, and the darkness has not overcome it.*

It's so simple and yet so profound. It refers to a time before Jesus was called Jesus. I don't know if he even had a name at that time. If he did, we're not told what that name was. So his best friend John simply called him "Word." It was a Greek philosophic term, but it was also a nickname. Words are invisible but powerful. That's who he was before he was called Jesus—invisible and powerful. If we were choosing a term today, perhaps we might call him "Password" because a password can access everything that is valuable and secret and important.

Back then—before the beginning, whatever we call him—he was with God, and he was God. And he was spectacular. He made everything. Everything that exists in the entire universe was created by him. And he is the light, the source of all life.

The truth is that our best human languages are not adequate to describe all that he was or what he was like. So we guess. We use our imagination and we describe him in our terms and in our experiences.

What must his heaven have been like around 5 BCE or 1 BCE? He was unquestionably the boss. Everyone in heaven knew him, and everyone in heaven adored him. An infinite number of angels constantly praised him for how good and great he was—and it wasn't flattery. He was absolutely worth it. And whatever he wanted he got. He could beckon an angel or simply speak with power. He was comfortable. He was invisible, so he could go anywhere at any time without any restrictions whatsoever. No one told him what to do. He was God. In our biggest thoughts and most extravagant speech, we cannot begin to describe him. It would be like a gnat trying to describe a galaxy, only a billion times more.

So how do we compare what it was like for him? Suppose you had a trillion dollars—more than you could ever spend. Imagine a house so large you couldn't visit all the rooms in a lifetime. Pretend that all your needs are satisfied. You are never sick, never tired or uncomfortable, never sad, never uninformed. Life is better than you ever imagined it could be.

Do I think it was like that for Jesus back before he was Jesus? No, not really. I think it was infinitely better. We can't really imagine how good it was. And then came Christmas.

Whatever he was called—let's call him the "Son of God" because that's what the Bible calls him—God the Father struck a deal with him that he would give all this up, leave heaven behind, and come to earth. Earth was this tiny little speck out there in one of the galaxies he had created, a place inhabited by human creatures that were in rebellion. And he would not only go there, but he would actually become a human. That's what the Bible tells us in John 1:14: *"The Word became flesh and made his dwelling among us."*

I doubt that the angels could comprehend how this could even be possible. While they had always believed that God could do anything, this seemed to be a stretch even for God. How does God shrink down to human size? How does God become a creature? And if he does become a creature, does that mean that he has to eat and sleep and go to the bathroom? And how long does all this humanity stuff last?

Actually, it was much more dramatic than even an angel could imagine.

The Son of God didn't shrink down to the size of a human but to the size of an embryo. God became microscopic. He lived for nine months inside a young virgin. The Light of the World was in complete darkness. The Word of God was silent. It was unimaginable.

What do you think of when you think of humility? Do you not think of someone who is great and powerful becoming a nobody? Is it not giving up fame, power and fortune? The New Testament says about Jesus in Philippians 2:6–7, *"Who, being in very nature God, did not consider equality with God something to be used to his own advantage, rather, he made himself nothing by taking the very nature of a servant, being made in human likeness."*

When he was born, he was named Jesus, but he was no less God. And so as God, but now human, he submitted to all the things that happen to humans—from birth to circumcision to being nursed at his mother's breast to having his diapers changed. He had to learn to talk, he who was the Word. He had to learn to walk, this Creator of the universe. He had to learn to feed himself, to read and write. He experienced the stuff of growing up from neighborhood bullies to puberty to learning a profession and making a living.

Was all this embarrassing? Humiliating? Infuriating? Amazingly, he did it all with dignity and grace. God became human—and not a human king but a human servant.

It takes my breath away. It kind of makes me wince. I want to look the other way. I am embarrassed. God should not have to be like me. But there's more. He not only humbled himself at Christmas but he humbled himself all the way to the cross.

I confess that my preference is to fight back when I think I'm right and others are wrong. I want to defend myself. I'm easily offended if my pride is hurt. I want to fight for my rights.

But, not Jesus! He let them laugh at him. He let them accuse him of things he had not done. He let them think they were better. He let them strip off his clothes. He let them beat him almost to death. They caused indescribable pain. They crucified him!

And he died. God died. The Creator of the universe, the Author of life, died! I don't know what it feels like to die, but Jesus did. I don't want to die, but Jesus volunteered to die. I want to die when I'm old and in my sleep, but Jesus died when he was young and on a public cross. I don't even like to think about it.

Jesus was God. Jesus was human. And Jesus was humble. I don't really get it, and I certainly don't have the vocabulary to explain it, but I am impressed beyond comprehension. Jesus was so great—so good—so humble.

Do you know the story of Edwin Hubble? The Hubble telescope is named after him. He was a truly astonishing man. In 1906 when he was a teenager, Hubble competed in an Illinois track meet and in one day won the pole vault, shot put, discus throw, hammer throw, standing high jump, and the running high jump. He was also on the winning mile-relay team. He won seven "First Place" ribbons in one track meet. He came in third in the broad jump and that same year set a record for the high jump in Illinois. He was one of the premier athletes in America.

Edwin was described as "handsome almost to a fault." They called him Adonis. He studied physics and astronomy at the University of Chicago and became one of the first Rhodes scholars at Oxford University.

He began his career as an astronomer at the Mount Wilson Observatory in California in 1919 at a time when astronomers believed that the Milky Way was the only galaxy. In 1924 he wrote a landmark paper showing that the universe contains many galaxies. He was the first to conceive that the universe is expanding. He basically changed the way scientists view the universe in which we live.

He was an amazing man, but for Edwin Hubble, none of that was enough. On his resume he claimed he was a successful lawyer in Kentucky in his 20s and 30s, but he lied; he taught school in Indiana. He bragged that he was a World War I hero. The truth is that he arrived in France one month before the Armistice was signed and probably never heard a shot fired. He told people stories about rescuing drowning swimmers. He never actually saved anyone. He claimed that he fought an exhibition fight with a world-class boxer and threw a knock-down punch. That fight never took place. Edwin Hubble was great but not humble. Jesus was God—and he was humble.

Jesus's whole life is a drama of humility. Between Christmas and the cross, he touched those that no one else would touch. He loved those that were unlovable. He embraced those that were the outcasts of society. He sided with the poor. He washed the feet of his followers. He honored women in a society that didn't.

Jesus is my hero. If there is anyone I want to be like, it's Jesus. Philippians 2:5–11 says:

In your relationships with one another, have the same attitude of mind Christ Jesus had: Who, being in very nature God, did not consider equality with God something to be used to his own advantage; rather, he made himself nothing by taking the very nature of a servant, being made in human likeness. And being found in appearance as a human being, he humbled himself by becoming obedient to death—even death on a cross. Therefore God exalted him to the highest place and gave him the name that is above every name, that at the name of Jesus every knee should bow, in heaven and on earth and under the earth, and every tongue acknowledge that Jesus Christ is Lord, to the glory of God the Father.

The promise and prediction of God the Father is that Jesus will be recognized by everyone everywhere. Jesus, even before he was given the name Jesus, trusted God the Father enough to turn over to him the keys of heaven. He surrendered the independent use of his divine powers and attributes. He left heaven, totally trusting that God the Father would take care of him and make everything right in the end.

Who do you trust to that extent? Who would you trust with power of attorney over all your assets or the PIN number for your credit card or bank card? Who would you trust with the keys to your house when you are outside alone on a sub-zero winter night? Who would you trust with the pages of your diary? Who would you allow to hypnotize you in front of a crowd?

Jesus trusted God the Father enough to give up everything, to serve others, and to suffer more than anyone before or since. He trusted God to make everything work out right in the end. And the Father guarantees him that one day the entire human race will know who Jesus is. One day everyone will give him the honor he deserves. One day *"at the name of Jesus every knee (will) bow, in heaven and on earth and under the earth, and every tongue acknowledge that Jesus Christ is Lord, to the glory of God the Father."*

The Missouri River is little more than a trickle at Three Forks, Montana, but it's a torrent at St. Louis where it meets up with the Mississippi River. You can step over the Mississippi in northern Minnesota, but at New Orleans the river flows at the rate of 600,000 cubic feet per second. What started small became great. Jesus started as God, humbled himself to a human trickle, and someday will be exalted beyond our imagination or description.

So what do we do with this picture of Jesus? Certainly we can learn about humility and seek to grow the same attitude as that of Christ Jesus. Surely we should be drawn to him as our Savior and Lord. But, most of all, let us just be impressed. See Jesus. Understand Jesus. Appreciate Jesus. Experience Jesus. He is so great—so good—so amazing—so wonderful—so humble.

Worship Through Giving

"Driven to Humility" by Christy Nockels, Eric Hill, Nathan Nockels (© 1997 Rocketown Music/Sweater Weather Music/HeeHee Music/Word Music, Inc. [Admin by Word Music Group, Inc.])

Key Lyrics: "I have been chosen to be driven to humility…to be wholly refined in your holy blaze of fire"

Resource: Listening CD—*Watermark*, by Watermark (2002, Rocketown Records).

Frequently we use the offering time as a moment of reflection and response. Immediately following the sermon, this song describes our struggle with humility and offers a plea to God for assistance in our journey towards humility.

Worship Through Music

"Sweet Mercies" by David Ruis (© 1995 Mercy/Vineyard Publishing/ASCAP)

Key Lyrics: "It's our confession Lord that we are weak…so very weak, but you are strong. And though we've nothing Lord to lay at your feet . . . we come to your feet and say help us along"

After singing the first verse and chorus, the worship leader can invite the congregation to confess to God the areas of their lives that have not been given to humility. The band can play through another verse and chorus quietly during the guided prayer.

Resource: Listening CD—*Every Move I Make*, by David Ruis (2004, Vineyard). Listening CD—*Heart of Worship*, by Worship-Together (available at www.grassrootsmusic.com). Listening CD—*Live From the 268 Generation*, by Passion Conferences (available at www.grassrootsmusic.com).

"We Fall Down" by Chris Tomlin (© 1998 Worshiptogether.com Songs/ASCAP)

Key Lyrics: "We fall down, we lay our crowns at the feet of Jesus"

Resource: Listening CD—*OneDay Live*, by Passion Conferences (2000, Sparrow, Emd). Listening CD—*Window to the Inner Court*, by Shane Everett (available at www.grassrootsmusic.com).

FaithStory

It is one thing to listen to songs and sermons on humility. It is a life transforming experience to hear real stories of how people came to faith in Jesus Christ by humbling themselves. Seek out members of your church that have faith stories to tell about their conversion to Christ and experience with humility. If their stories of conversion do not have strong ties to the humility theme, you may consider having them share briefly about their conversion experience and give more time and attention to life experiences that have taught them humility.

Worship Through Music

"The Wonderful Cross" original words by Isaac Watts, original music by Lowell Mason (Public domain), additional refrain by Chris Tomlin, J.D. Walt, and Jesse Reeves (© 2000 Worshiptogether.com/Six Steps Publishing)

> Key Lyrics: "My richest gain I count but loss and pour contempt on all my pride"

> Video Option: At the end of the song, show an image of a cross on screens while the band plays an extended instrumental ending. If you have the capabilities, a moving flash image of a cross would add a special dynamic as people reflect on the message of the cross of Jesus Christ as a motivating factor in their decision to seek humility.

> Resource: Listening CD—*Song Discovery Volume 25* (available at www.songdiscovery.com). Listening CD—*The Noise We Make,* by Chris Tomlin (available at www.grassrootsmusic.com). Printed music at www.songdiscovery.com.

> This is the classic hymn "When I Survey the Wondrous Cross" adapted for contemporary settings with a new chorus added that adds the challenge, "O the wonderful cross bids me come and die and find that I may truly live."

Benediction

For you know the grace of our Lord Jesus Christ, that though he was rich, yet for your sake he became poor, so that you through his poverty might become rich. Amen. (2 Corinthians 8:9)

TRADITIONAL WORSHIP MUSIC OPTIONS:

Call to Worship Choir Anthem

"Christus Paradox" by Dunstan/Arr. Fedak (©1991 GIA Publications, Inc.)

> Key Lyrics: "You, Lord, are both Lamb and Shepherd . . . You, Lord, are both prince and slave"

Feature Choir Anthem

"Offertory" by John Ness Beck (© 1987 Beckenhorst Press, Inc.)

Key Lyrics: "And what does the Lord require of you but to do justice and to love kindness and to walk humbly ... walk humbly with your God?"

Hymn Options

"Praise to the Lord, the Almighty" by Joachim Neander, Catherine Winkworth, Paul Schilling, and Rupert Davies (Public domain)

Key Lyrics: "Ponder anew what the Almighty can do if with his love he befriend thee"

"Jesus Came, the Heavens Adoring" words by Godfrey Thring, music by John Goss (Public domain)

Key Lyrics: "Jesus came for our redemption ... humbly came on earth to die"

"My Lord, You Wore No Royal Crown" words by Christopher Idle (© 1982 Hope Publishing Company)

Key Lyrics: "You came unequaled, undeserved to be what we were meant to be ... to serve, instead of being served a light for all the world to see

"O God, Who Gives To Humankind" by Burns, Tallis (Public domain)

Key Lyrics: "As knowledge grows, Lord, keep us free from self-destructive vanity"

"And Can It Be That I Should Gain" words by Charles Wesley, music by Thomas Campbell (Public domain)

Key Lyrics: "'Tis mystery all! The Immortal dies who can explore his strange design"

"May the Mind of Christ My Savior" words by Kate Wilkinson, music by A. Cyril Barham-Gould (Public domain)

Key Lyrics: "May the mind of Christ my Savior live in me from day to day by his love and power controlling all I do and say"

Service 2

Overcoming Temptations

THEME

Temptation

BIBLE PASSAGES

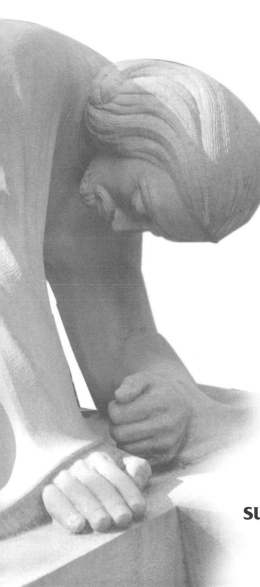

Hebrews 2:18
Because he himself suffered when he was tempted, he is able to help those who are being tempted.

Hebrews 4:15–16
For we do not have a high priest who is unable to empathize with our weaknesses, but we have one who has been tempted in every way, just as we are—yet he did not sin. Let us then approach God's throne of grace with confidence, so that we may receive mercy and find grace to help us in our time of need.

Matthew 4:1–11
Then Jesus was led by the Spirit into the wilderness to be tempted by the devil. After fasting forty days and forty nights, he was hungry. The tempter came to him and said, "If you are the Son of God, tell these stones to become bread." Jesus answered, "It is written: 'People do not live on bread alone, but on every word that comes from the mouth of God.'" Then the devil took him to the holy city and had him stand on the highest point of the temple. "If you are the Son of God," he said, "throw yourself down. For it is written: 'He will command his angels concerning you, and they will lift you up in their hands, so that you will not strike your foot against a stone.'" Jesus answered him, "It is also written: 'Do not put the Lord your God to the test.'" Again, the devil took him to a very high mountain and showed him all the kingdoms of the world and their splendor. "All this I will give you," he said, "if you will bow down and worship me." Jesus said to him, "Away from me, Satan! For it is written: 'Worship the Lord your God, and serve him only.'" Then the devil left him, and angels came and attended him.

SUMMARY

Jesus received personal attention when Satan tried to tempt him into sin. The temptations were real and enticing, but Jesus chose to resist the devil and avoid sin. From Jesus's example we learn about our own vulnerability and how to resist temptation. With Jesus's help we have strength from a Lord who personally understands how hard temptations can be.

SERVICE IMAGE

The DVD features a graphic image suitable for use during the "Overcoming Temptations" service. This suggested worship background is a photograph of a rocky cliff. This worship background appears on the *Abingdon Worship Photos, vol 3: Projection Images for Lent and Easter,* by Jim and Mary Whitmer (2003, Abingdon).

CONTEMPORARY SERVICE SEQUENCE:

Prelude

"Cry of My Heart" by Terry Butler, Arranged by John Carlson (© 1992 Vineyard Ministries International. Administered by Music Services.)

Resource: Listening CD—*Willow Creek Preludes: Volume 1.* Lyrics, video, demo track, rehearsal track, and printed music at www.willowcreek.com/resources/music.asp. (Search for "Cry of My Heart" or use the following url—http://www.willowcreek.com/ arrangement.asp?action=details&invtid=PR19164&arrangementid=130 3&sid=12)

This instrumental is a jazz/rock version of the congregational chorus featuring saxophone on the melody.

Worship Through Music

"O for a Thousand Tongues to Sing" words by Charles Wesley, music by Carl G. Glaser, arr. by Lowell Mason (Public domain)

Key Lyrics: "He breaks the power of canceled sin . . . He sets the prisoner free"

Stylistic variation: This traditional hymn can be performed in either a traditional or contemporary manner. Here is an example of a contemporary version that slightly alters the melody:

"Hallelujah" (Your Love is Amazing) by Brenton Brown (© 2000 Vineyard Songs [UK/Erie])

Key Lyrics: "When I am surrounded your love carries me"

Resource: Listening CD—*Surrender*, by Vineyard Music (available at www.grassrootsmusic.com). Listening CD—*Be Glorified*, by Worship-Together (2003, Time Life Records). Printed music at www.praisecharts.com.

"I Believe In Jesus" by Marc Nelson (© 1987 Mercy Publishing)

Key Lyrics: "I believe you're here now . . . here with the power to heal now…and the grace to forgive"

Resource: Listening CD—*WOW Worship* (2000, Sony). Listening CD—*Change My Heart Oh God* (1996, Vineyard).

Welcome

The worship leader can use this time to have everyone in the congregation greet one another and then, after seating them, briefly introduce the week's theme of temptation. A good option is to tell a brief but lighthearted story about temptation that everyone can relate to. For example: temptation to eat too much at the state fair, drive too fast to an appointment, or cut in line at the grocery store. After the brief, humorous story, a key emotional pivot needs to set up the drama, which is a serious look at the kind of temptations that destroy individuals and their relationships.

Worship Through Drama

(Please view the drama on the resource DVD. The drama is available as both a performance and a script.)

THE PROMISED DELIVERY
(Written by Shelly Barsuhn)

Characters/cast:	ANTHONY
	SHADOW
	BRIDGET

Props:	Chair
	Lamp
	Scrap of paper

Costume:	Anthony—Comfort clothes (loungewear, sweats, etc.)
	Bridget—Pajamas and robe
	Shadow—Dark clothing, nondescript

(*ANTHONY is sitting in a chair, his head in his hands. SHADOW stands behind him. BRIDGET enters. She watches ANTHONY for a moment. It is obvious that he is in distress.*)

BRIDGET: Anthony?

ANTHONY: (*not wanting to be disturbed*) What are you doing up? It's late. Go to bed.

BRIDGET: I was worried about you.

SHADOW: You're checking up on me.

ANTHONY: I was just going to check the computer. See if we have any mail.

BRIDGET: Why can't that wait until tomorrow?

ANTHONY: (*insistently*) Just go to bed.

BRIDGET: I worry when you're—alone.

ANTHONY: That doesn't help. It just makes me feel guilty. Listen, I'm trying. That's all I can do.

BRIDGET: And that's all I can ask. Just don't put yourself in the way of temptation. Will you come up soon?

ANTHONY: Yes.

BRIDGET/
SHADOW: Really?

ANTHONY: (*turning toward her, sharply*) Yes!

BRIDGET: (*taken aback*) Sorry.

(*ANTHONY cringes in remorse. BRIDGET starts to exit. ANTHONY reaches for her unwilling hand. BRIDGET is not angry—just fearful.*)

ANTHONY: No, I'm sorry. I didn't mean to—

SHADOW: You said you wouldn't take your frustration out on Bridget any more. It's your problem, not hers. Don't blame her.

BRIDGET: (*retreating*) I'll just go up…

ANTHONY: No. Wait. (*He catches her hand. She looks down at her hand in his. He drops hers.*) Please. I need you to understand. I have these questions running in my brain—that's why I jumped on you. Hearing you is like a big echo. "Can you do this? Really?" (*very frustrated*) Exactly what I'm asking myself. I want to—so badly.

SHADOW: Then do it!

ANTHONY: I'm trying!

BRIDGET: I know!

SHADOW: Resist the temptation.

ANTHONY: I don't just want to resist it, I want to smash it! *(to BRIDGET)* You're right to question. I don't trust me, either.

BRIDGET: *(tenderly)* So I don't trust you ... yet ... I believe you can do it.

             (SHADOW and ANTHONY respond to this outreach.)

BRIDGET: *(repeating herself to get him to comprehend)* I believe you can do it.

             (BRIDGET embraces ANTHONY. She pulls a paper out of her pocket, unfolds it, and shows it to ANTHONY.)

BRIDGET: I wrote this down.

             (ANTHONY looks at the paper, reading silently.)

SHADOW: "Be on your guard; stand firm in the faith; be courageous; be strong."

BRIDGET: It's from First Corinthians.
             Naïve, huh. Simplistic.

ANTHONY: It's not naïve.

SHADOW: I'll keep it with me. *(SHADOW touches his head.)*

BRIDGET: I'm not being too preachy? I don't want to be preachy.

ANTHONY: *(teasing)* You're a little preachy, but I'll get over it...eventually.

BRIDGET: *(surprised and touched)* You sounded like your old self just then.

             (They smile, enjoying the moment.)

SHADOW: I am sorry, Bridget. So sorry for everything. I'll never be able to make it up to you, what I've put you through.

BRIDGET: Come to bed.

             (BRIDGET exits. ANTHONY watches her go. As soon as she has disappeared—)

SHADOW: She has no idea what I'm dealing with. How powerful. But she's trying. She's trying so hard.

(ANTHONY goes back to the chair and sits down. He clenches his fists in utter frustration and groans.)

ANTHONY: I want to be strong. But it is almost impossible. (He drops his head into his hands.)

SHADOW: *(resolving)* But not impossible.

ANTHONY: I can resist.

SHADOW: Right now.

ANTHONY: Any time. Tomorrow, even.

SHADOW: Right now.

ANTHONY: "Now it is required that those who have been given a trust must prove faithful." If it weren't so hard.

SHADOW: "Watch and pray so that you will not fall into temptation."

ANTHONY: I remember that.

SHADOW: "Be careful to obey all that is written in the Book of the Law of Moses, without turning aside to the right or to the left."
"He is the Rock, his works are perfect."

ANTHONY: Oh, God—

SHADOW: "Know therefore that the LORD your God is God . . ."

ANTHONY: "For the word of the LORD is right and true; he is faithful in all he does."

SHADOW: "And lead us not into temptation, but deliver us from the evil one."

ANTHONY: I am so tired.

SHADOW: Go to bed.
One more day.

(Freeze. Exit.)

Worship Through Teaching

OVERCOMING TEMPTATION
Hebrews 4:15; 2:16–18, Matthew 4:1–11

You know that thirty-something who is obsessed with pornography? He seems to be on a never-ending and never-satisfying journey through the one and a half million pornographic websites that are available on the Internet. If you listen to his soul, it will whisper a secret you may not know.

You know that couple who is always trying to get more? Their lives seem to be totally defined in terms of things. They are always buying what they cannot afford. They define themselves and their worth by designer logos, expensive cars, and an overpriced home. If you listen carefully to their souls, they will whisper something you may have never expected.

You know that woman who is always in your face? She always has a complaint, is easily angered, is a real grouch, and is just overbearing and demanding. As much as you don't want to listen to anything else she ever has to say, it might be good to listen to the quiet voice that speaks from deep inside of her.

You know your friend who drinks too much? He showed up drunk at your party. He said he would come to your son's basketball game, but he didn't show up. He said it would never happen again, but he just got another DWI. Have you ever heard the whisper of his heart?

It is the same whisper in all of those hearts. It's a whisper in so many of our souls. It says, "This is not who I want to be! I don't want to be unkind. I don't want to be greedy. I don't want to be controlled by pornography. I don't want to be an addict. I don't want to be a grouch. I don't want to lie. But I have caved in to temptation so many times that I have turned into someone I never wanted to become.

As we are looking in the mirror and seeing what we do not wish to see, Jesus appears behind us. Some of us are embarrassed. Some of us are defensive. Some of us feel judged and want to run away because his being there makes us feel so guilty. We know we have failed so many times. We just don't want Jesus there. But Jesus isn't there to judge. He's there to help. As strange as it may seem, he understands. He really does understand. We are told in Hebrews 2:18, "Because he himself suffered when he was tempted, he is able to help those who are being tempted." And adding to that in Hebrews 4:15–16 we read:

> *For we do not have a high priest who is unable to empathize with our weaknesses, but we have one [Jesus the Son of God] who has been tempted in every way, just as we are—yet he did not sin. Let us then approach God's throne of grace with confidence, so that we may receive mercy and find grace to help us in our time of need.*

When it comes to this whole issue of temptation and caving into temptation, let me tell you up front that I am not here to criticize failures or condemn bad habits. I will not exhort you to avoid temptations to sin. I just want to tell you about Jesus.

When Jesus was about 30 years old, he faced 40 of the toughest days of his entire life. For six weeks he lived alone in the Judean wilderness and didn't eat. It's a desolate place, the Judean wilderness, with few inhabitants, little water, scorching heat, and lots of rocks. Let's read what happened in Matthew 4:1–11:

Then Jesus was led by the Spirit into the wilderness to be tempted by the devil. After fasting forty days and forty nights, he was hungry. The tempter came to him and said, "If you are the Son of God, tell these stones to become bread." Jesus answered, "It is written: 'People do not live on bread alone, but on every word that comes from the mouth of God.'" Then the devil took him to the holy city and had him stand on the highest point of the temple. "If you are the Son of God," he said, "throw yourself down. For it is written: 'He will command his angels concerning you, and they will lift you up in their hands, so that you will not strike your foot against a stone.'" Jesus answered him, "It is also written: 'Do not put the Lord your God to the test.'" Again, the devil took him to a very high mountain and showed him all the kingdoms of the world and their splendor. "All this I will give you," he said, "if you will bow down and worship me." Jesus said to him, "Away from me, Satan! For it is written: 'Worship the Lord your God, and serve him only.'" Then the devil left him, and angels came and attended him.

It all started really well. Jesus was a good person seeking to do the right thing. He went into the desert because he was led there by the Holy Spirit. I don't know if Jesus had any idea where the Spirit was leading him. My guess is that he didn't have any idea what he was getting himself into. So often we assume that if we are good people and are led by the Holy Spirit, life will be easy. Hardly ever do we think that the Holy Spirit of God will lead us to a place where we will encounter the devil.

Jesus didn't eat for almost 1000 hours. Some of us say we are starved if we don't eat for four hours! He went without food for 40 days and 40 nights. Fasting has always been an important spiritual discipline for godly people and there are multiple reasons to explain Jesus's unusually long fast. Whatever the reason, it is surprising he survived.

A healthy 30-year-old male in the present-day United States consumes about 4000 calories per day. But let's assume that Jesus needed only 2500 calories per day to maintain his body weight. That would mean that in 40 days and 40 nights he would lose 40 pounds. If he started out weighing 150 pounds, then at the end of almost six weeks, his weight would have dropped to 110 pounds or less. He must have been starving to death—literally.

Deserts are hot and dry. Water is difficult to get. While Jesus must have had water to drink during those six weeks, it would have been a constant challenge to stay hydrated. (I once rode in a truck that broke down south of the Sahara Desert along the border between Burkina Faso and Mali. It was 120 to 130 degrees in the shade. In an hour my skin was dry, and the beginning effects of dehydration were evident. Constant drinking never seemed to be enough.)

All of this is to say that Jesus was weak and weary when Satan launched his first temptation. Perhaps you could say that it is a satanic strategy to attack during weakness and vulnerability. But maybe that's not the answer. Perhaps it is just life. Maybe it's just that there is no good time to face life's hardest issues or highest temptations.

At least in Jesus' story it seems that Satan's suggestion was reasonable and simple. "The tempter came to him and said, 'If you are the Son of God, tell these stones to become bread.'"

Certainly there is nothing wrong with a hungry man getting a loaf of bread to eat. And there is no sin in Jesus performing a miracle. Often in Jesus' story we are told about him eating bread, and twice he miraculously made bread for hungry thousands to eat. And, if nothing else, this was an acknowledgement by the devil that Jesus had the supernatural power to turn some of the limestone rocks that are scattered throughout the Judean wilderness into loaves of bread.

Jesus must have wanted to do it. I can't imagine him not wanting to. What would you do? Wouldn't you perform a miracle and eat the bread?

So, then, why wouldn't Jesus? Apparently, Jesus did not want to be controlled by anyone who was evil. It was an interesting situation, this whole issue of not letting someone who is evil make him do a good thing, of not allowing Satan to get his pitchfork in the door, of not taking orders from anyone but God. Jesus—even though he was hungry and tired and weary—would not allow a physical need to take precedence over his spiritual need. And so he answered, *It is written: 'People do not live on bread alone.'*

I think Jesus wanted to, but he didn't. It's hard to say "no" to what feels good when you are sick and tired. It's hard to do what is right when there seems to be such a fine line between right and wrong.

After 40 days, Jesus must have been a whole lot more than hungry. He must have been lonely. Some people start feeling desperate after 40 minutes. Can you imagine being alone for 40 days? Not even prisons keep inmates in solitary confinement that long lest they go mad.

Jesus was a people-person. He was always surrounded by a crowd. He talked to people and touched them. He sat with them and sailed with them. He loved to ask questions, to teach truth, to hang out, and just to be with people. After 40 days alone, even Satan must have looked good as someone to talk with.

It is amazing how vulnerable to temptation we can be when we are lonely. Lonely people sometimes make awful choices—choices they would never make in a more rational moment—just to be touched, just to be talked to, just to be acknowledged. Lonely people sleep with people that they should never have been with. Lonely people commit crimes that run against every value they have ever espoused. Lonely people will join a gang or tell a lie just to be loved, accepted, or popular. Some even choose a lifetime in a desperate and difficult marriage rather than be alone and lonely outside of marriage.

Satan tempted Jesus with popularity at his loneliest moment. He took Jesus on a quick trip from the desert to the city of Jerusalem to visit the Temple. The Temple was actually one of the amazing wonders of the ancient world. It was a magnificent structure made of white marble and decorated with glistening gold. Satan took him to a place called the pinnacle. From the high point of the pinnacle of the Temple to the bottom of the Kidron Valley was 450 feet. That's 45 stories. Satan offered a deal to Jesus:

> *"If you are the Son of God," he said, "throw yourself down. For it is written: 'He will command his angels concerning you, and they will lift you up in their hands, so that you will not strike your foot against a stone.'"*

It was a second compliment. If you are the Son of God, you can perform a miracle to create bread. If you are the Son of God, you are going to be safe because God is going to take care of you. And Jesus must have wanted to do it. If he had jumped off the Temple, it would have proven he was the Son of God. That was a lesson Satan needed to learn. Jesus could have freefallen toward the people who had gathered to watch what appeared to be a suicide jump and then have had angels swoop in at the last minute to save him before he hit. The crowd would have been dazzled and would have applauded. They would have wanted to touch him and be near him and talk to him. He would have been the center of attention. No longer would he have been lonely. It sounds like a plan!

Do you ever get that "I'll show them" feeling? You know: "I'm going to teach the bad guys a lesson!" Jesus must have felt that way. But instead, "Jesus answered him, *"It is also written: 'Do not put the Lord your God to the test.'"*

Jesus didn't need to prove anything. He was the Son of God whether he took the plunge or not. I'm afraid I would have jumped. But Jesus didn't.

Then came what may have been the toughest test of the three, recorded in Matthew 4:8–9:

> *Again the devil took him to a very high mountain and showed him all the kingdoms of the world and their splendor. "All this I will give you," he said, "if you will bow down and worship me."*

Here was an offer that must have been exceptionally difficult to refuse. You know the frequent question about why God allows all the problems in our world. If there is a God, why does crime exist? If there is a God, why do young children become sick and die? If God really is loving and powerful, why are there earthquakes and tidal waves and wars and terrorists? Why are there all these things if there really is a God? Here Satan offers a deal to Jesus, and the deal is for Jesus to rule the world and get rid of all these things.

Actually, this offer was in keeping with Jesus's goal in life. He cared deeply about people. His mission was to save our world from the consequences of sin. The plan was for him to die on the cross, but here was a very desirable and much easier way.

The problem was that Satan demanded worship as a prerequisite. Worship acknowledges superiority. Jesus must have thought about saying yes. But it would have been a disaster if he did. It was an example of the end justifying the means. The truth is that it never would have worked. Satan would have accepted the worship and kept the rule of the world for himself. God can be trusted to keep his word, but Satan cannot. And so Jesus said, *"Away from me, Satan! For it is written: 'Worship the Lord your God, and serve him only.'"*

So, what is the point of all of this? The point is that Jesus knows what it is like to be tempted when weary, when lonely, and when caring enough to want to do good for other people. The point is that he struggled with doing the wrong thing and decided to do the right thing. The point is that he understands our struggles with decisions and temptations.

Maybe you are thinking, "No, he doesn't. There is not an outside chance that he could really understand, so don't tell me he does. Don't tell me that Jesus understands the pressure at school to take drugs or to have sex. Don't tell me that Jesus knows what I feel when I need one more drink or four more pills in order to get through one more day. Don't tell me that he comes close to understanding how much I hate the person who has hurt me so deeply. Don't tell me he feels my depression or thoughts about taking my own life. Don't tell me that he knows about the abuse I've suffered and the thoughts I think."

That is exactly what I'm telling you. Jesus, the Son of God, has been tempted in every way, just as we are. He is not our critic; he is our cheerleader. He is not our enemy; he's our friend. He is not our judge; he's our defender. He's not out to get us; he's on our side.

When we click the mouse, when we touch the liquor bottle, when we feel the greed, when we don't want to forgive, when we want to get even, when we feel like lying, when we are ready to steal, when we want to cheat, when the temptation is so strong it is like gravity itself pulling us into sin, Jesus is there—Jesus understands—Jesus is on our side, saving us from sin.

Worship Through Giving

"You Alone" by Kim Hill, Jamie Kenney, Judie Lawson (© 1998 Pretty Feet Music/King Garf Music/Pyewacket Frog)

Key Lyrics: "So I won't fear though darkness hides me. No I won't let my courage sway for you are near and at the brightness of your glory the shadows of the night melt away"

Resource: Listening CD—*Song Discovery Vol 13* (available at www.songdiscovery.com). Printed music at www.songdiscovery.com.

Pastoral Prayer

Our father we acknowledge that in you our needs are met. In you we find the ultimate satisfaction and the understanding that you love us and are concerned about even the smallest details of our lives. We pray for your blessing on each of these, your people. We confess to you our sins and acknowledge that we have often done what we should not have done. Or not done what we should have. Forgive our sins. Give to us the cleansing that you alone can give through Jesus.

God I pray for your touch on the bodies of each of these that commit themselves to you. For those that struggle with illness of the mind and maladies of the soul I pray for encouragement, help, and hope. I also pray for your blessing upon families that have special needs and are estranged from each other. For marriages that are teetering, that you will give them strength and stability.

God, whatever the need is listen to the hearts of these that pray here and intervene. We commit ourselves to the truth of your love and the power of Jesus Christ. We commit all that we are and all that we are about to you. In the name of Jesus Christ…amen.

Worship Through Music

"Breathe" by Marie Barnett (© 1995 Mercy/Vineyard)

Key Lyrics: "I'm desperate for you . . . I'm lost without you"

Resource: Listening CD—*Breathe*, by Vineyard Music (2003, Vineyard Music). Listening CD—*Hungry*, by Vineyard Music (2001, Vineyard Music).

"In Christ Alone" by Shawn Craig & Don Koch (© 1990 Paragon Music Corp.)

Key Lyrics: "In Christ alone I place my trust and find my glory in the power of the cross. In every victory let it be said of me my source of strength, my source of hope is Christ alone."

Resource: Listening CD—*Songs4Worship, volume 20* (Time Life Music and Integrity Music).

FaithStory

It is difficult to find a person that will share about struggling with temptation; however, this is an opportunity to have a leader of an addiction-support-ministry share his or her faith story. It would be appropriate for this person to describe some aspect of the ministry and its effectiveness. It is essential to have a mature Christian do this so as to speak appropriately about the temptations of addicts.

Worship Through Music

"I Walk By Faith" by Chris Falson (© 1990,1999 Maranatha Praise, Inc.)

Key Lyrics: "I walk by faith each step by faith . . . to live by faith I put my trust in you"

Resource: Listening CD—*WOW Worship Orange* (2000, Sony).

Benediction

God is faithful; he will not let you be tempted beyond what you can bear. But when you are tempted, he will also provide a way out so that you can endure it. (1 Corinthians 10:13)

TRADITIONAL WORSHIP MUSIC OPTIONS:

Feature Choir Anthem

"O How Amiable" by Ralph Vaughan Williams (1940, Oxford University Press)

Key Lyrics: "O God, our help in ages past . . . our hope for years to come . . . our shelter from the stormy blast . . . and our eternal home"

Hymn Options

"A Mighty Fortress Is Our God" by Martin Luther, tr. Frederick Hedge (Public domain)

Key Lyrics: "And though this world, with devils filled should threaten to undo us we will not fear, for God hath willed his truth to triumph through us"

"God of Grace and God of Glory" words by Harry Emerson Fosdick, music by John Hughes (Public domain)

> Key Lyrics: "God of grace and God of glory on your people pour your power . . . Grant us wisdom grant us courage"

"Christian Do You Struggle?" by Neale, Polman, Dykes (© 1987 CEC Publications.)

> Key Lyrics: "Christian, do not tremble, do not be downcast, arm yourself for battle watch and pray and fast"

"I Need Thee Every Hour" words by Annie S. Hawks, music by Robert Lowry (Public domain)

> Key Lyrics: "I need thee every hour, stay thou near by, temptations lose their power when thou art nigh"

"O Jesus I Have Promised" words by John E. Bode, music by Arthur H. Mann (Public domain)

> Key Lyrics: "My foes are ever near me, around me and within . . . but, Jesus, draw thou nearer and shield my soul from sin"

Service 3

Making Friends

THEME

Discipleship

BIBLE PASSAGES

Matthew 4:18–20
As Jesus was walking beside the Sea of Galilee, he saw two brothers, Simon called Peter and his brother Andrew. They were casting a net into the lake, for they were fishermen. "Come, follow me," Jesus said, "and I will make you fishers of people." At once they left their nets and followed him.

Luke 6:12–16
One of those days Jesus went out to a mountainside to pray, and spent the night praying to God. When morning came, he called his disciples to him and chose twelve of them whom he also designated apostles: Simon (whom he named Peter), his brother Andrew, James, John, Philip, Bartholomew, Matthew, Thomas, James son of Alphaeus, Simon who was called the Zealot, Judas son of James, and Judas Iscariot, who became a traitor.

Matthew 28:19–20
Therefore go and make disciples of all nations, baptizing them in the name of the Father and the Son and of the Holy Spirit, and teaching them to obey everything that I have commanded you. And surely I am with you always, to the very end of the age.

John 15:13–16
Greater love has no one than this, to lay down one's life for one's friends. You are my friends if you do what I command . . . I have called you friends, for everything that I learned from my Father I have made known to you. You did not choose me, but I chose you.

SUMMARY

We call them apostles or disciples, and we name books of the Bible, church buildings, and cities after them. But they were also simply Jesus's friends. Jesus wanted and needed human friends. He calls us to be his friends, his disciples, and his disciple makers.

SERVICE IMAGE

The DVD features a graphic image suitable for use during the "Making Friends" service. This suggested worship background shows several friends together. This worship background is taken from the video that SpiritFilms™ created for this service.

VIDEO

The DVD also features a video clip suitable for use during the "Making Friends" service. This suggested video may be used at any point during the service.

CONTEMPORARY SERVICE SEQUENCE:

Prelude

"Sweeter" by Cindy Cruse-Ratcliff, Israel Houghton, Meleasa Houton (© 2003 Champions For Christ Music Publishing/Integrity's Praise! Music/Lakewood Ministries /My Other Publishing Company/Sound of The New Breed.)

Key Lyrics: "What a privilege to know you like I know you…to be loved like you love me"

Resource: Listening CD—*iWORSHIP Next (*2004, Sony). Printed music at www.praisecharts.com.

This song works well as a prelude in that it features the vocals and the band with an up-tempo song. The melody is memorable, and the lyrics discuss the theme of relational intimacy with God. Using a congregational song as a prelude is one effective way to teach new songs that will later be used in the normal flow of a service.

Worship Through Music

"Jesus, Lover of My Soul" by Daniel Grul, John Ezzy, Steve McPherson (©1998 Daniel Grul, John Ezzy, Steve McPherson [Hillsong])

Key Lyrics: "My Savior, my closest Friend…I will worship you until the very end"

Resource: Listening CD—*iWORSHIP, vol 2* (Integrity). Printed music at www.praisecharts.com.

Welcome

This week of the series would be a good time to launch small groups as a part of a discipleship initiative. Also, provide any information about various Lent activities that provide opportunities for discipleship.

Worship Through Drama

(Please view the drama on the resource DVD; the drama is available as both a performance and a script.)

RELATIONSHIP IN WAITING
(Written by Shelly Barsuhn)

Characters/cast: JAY, gentle but charismatic man
JOHN, a friend
CHRIS, a former friend

Props: Shopping bags (many)
Purse
Pocket calendar or Filofax
Cell phone

(JAY enters and crosses stage at a leisurely pace. JOHN enters, sees JAY.)

JOHN: Jay! Hey, Jay!

JAY: John! Good to see you!

(They meet, greeting one another enthusiastically. It is obvious they are very good friends.)

JOHN: Are we still getting together for dinner tonight?

JAY: Of course. Wouldn't miss it.

JOHN: Fantastic. I have so much to tell you . . . ask you. Until then.

JAY: I look forward to it!

(They part. JOHN exits. JAY's cell phone rings. He checks caller ID and smiles.)

JAY: Hi, Barb. . . . Caller ID, of course. It's a wonderful thing . . . No, you're not being a pest. I want to hear from you. . . . Sure I'd love to meet him. Bring him over. . . . Any friend of yours is bound to be a friend of mine. Tomorrow, okay? Say 10:00. . . . Great. I am so glad you called. . . . See you soon.

(JAY closes phone. CHRIS enters, loaded down with shopping bags. She fumbles and drops one bag. It lands heavily. JAY hurries to help.)

JAY: *(handing her the bag)* There you go.

CHRIS: *(taking bag)* Thanks.

(CHRIS moves to continue, then stops.)

I know you.

(JAY pauses.)

CHRIS: Can't quite put my finger on it.

(JAY shrugs, good-natured.)

CHRIS: Wait a minute. Jay?

JAY: Yes.

CHRIS: Jay! I can't believe it's you!

It's me. Chris. Chris Burnon. We met—oh, it's been years, now.

(JAY still looks bewildered.)

Come on, it hasn't been that long.

JAY: I am so sorry. How embarrassing. I don't usually forget . . .

CHRIS: It's my fault. I haven't been in touch. I've been meaning to call or connect, somehow. I do think about you every now and again.

JAY: That's a start, I suppose.

CHRIS: I don't know why, but even though we haven't seen each other, I still think of you as a friend.

JAY: Okay . . .

CHRIS: And I guess the only way you'll be able to say the same about me is if I give you a call now and then.

JAY: That would be good. My friends are very important to me.

CHRIS: I know! I had never met anyone like you. You really connected with people. It's a gift. It would be fun to get to know you again.

JAY: Well . . . Do you have a moment right now? *(He sits down on the step.)* We can sit down for a second and catch up . . .

CHRIS: I would love to—but I can't. Not right now. *(sudden idea:)* I can call you. *(She gets calendar out of her purse)* Next week. I just have to get through this hectic week. I'm sure next Thursday I'll have a minute. Certainly by Friday. I think I still have your number.

JAY: *(standing)* All right. I'll wait to hear from you.

CHRIS: Great. Wonderful to bump into you. I'll be thinking about you.

JAY: All right . . .

CHRIS: Bye, then. Thanks. See you.

JAY: Hope to.

(CHRIS exits. JAY watches, then exits.)

Worship Through Teaching

MAKING FRIENDS
Matthew 4:18–20; Luke 6:12–16; Matthew 28:19–20; John 15:13–16

My family moved twice during my growing up years—when I was in first grade and again when I was in seventh grade. Changing homes and schools was difficult, but the hardest part was making new friends. It was especially difficult in junior high when we moved to a town of about 5000 where almost everyone in my class had known each other all their lives. I was both scared and excited. I wanted to make friends but didn't quite know how to go about it.

We all need friends, you know. Even Jesus needed friends. Not just crowds of people who would applaud him but friends who would like him for himself. He wanted other people to hang out with, to relax with and to just be his friends.

You probably know that he gathered a dozen people around him and called them disciples. We often talk about them with a measure of awe and call them saints. In books and sermons we are told that we, too, should be disciples—followers of Jesus. Maybe we have wondered what it was like to be Peter or Andrew or James. But, seldom do we think of the relationship from Jesus' side.

We often talk as if Jesus recruited his twelve disciples like an NCAA Division One basketball coach picking winners to take him to the championships, or the CEO of a Fortune 100 company building a top-flight management team. We think of Jesus choosing people he could later use to spread his message or write his Bible and build his church. While there is validity in this, let's look at Jesus and his disciples from a different angle today—that of a thirty-something man from Nazareth who simply wanted to make some friends.

Some people seem to be so "together." They seem so self-confident and self-sufficient that they don't much need anyone else. It seems to me that Jesus was the most "together" person who ever lived. He always knew what to say. He always handled difficult situations with brilliant creativity. He faced difficulty with extraordinary grace. So, it is something of a surprise to discover that he wanted a group of a dozen friends. Not that they were his only friends, but apparently they were his closest friends.

Let's go back to one day when Jesus was alone—and perhaps lonely. Some say that loneliness is a universal human experience. Everybody at one point or another in life is lonely, and Jesus certainly was not exempt from those feelings. Loneliness is that sense that you are totally on your own, that no one else understands or cares, that there is no one to whom you can turn for help, and that you have to take care of everything by yourself. Loneliness sometimes comes in the midst of overwhelming problems, but it can also follow unprecedented success. Loneliness can last for a minute, or it can last for a lifetime.

Jesus's time of loneliness came on a day that was full of success and criticism. He was teaching in the synagogue where he had grown up, so it was an honored occasion for him. No doubt his heart was pumping with excitement over this opportunity. But there were critics in the congregation who confronted him and argued with him over a fine point of Jewish law. There was at the synagogue that day a man whose right hand was disabled. Jesus wanted to use his supernatural power to heal that man, but his critics insisted that it would be disobedient to God to heal him on the Sabbath because it could wait until the next morning. Jesus believed it was the right thing to do, so he decided to go ahead and heal him anyway, but his critics were so outraged that they conspired to hurt him. Jesus needed to get away, so he went off by himself.

The biographer Luke says in Luke 6:12 that *"Jesus went out to a mountainside to pray, and spent the night praying to God."* We are not told the content of that all-night prayer, but from it we learn some lessons that we don't always understand. As a first resort when Jesus was under stress and in the midst of loneliness, he went to God the Father. It was not a last resort. We also learn that prayer should precede our problem solving, not follow it, and that walking away from a busy schedule and spending a night in prayer can be the first and best strategy when life is hard.

We don't know what Jesus prayed about, and we don't know what God said. But we do know what Jesus did, and can probably guess what God said. God told him to go and make some friends. If he was going to make his life count, if he was going to survive his critics, if he was going to help others, then Jesus shouldn't be alone. He needed to make some friends. It was a father telling his son, "Go and make some friends."

Biographer Luke goes on to say:

> When morning came, he called his disciples to him and choose twelve of them, whom he also designated apostles: Simon (whom he named Peter), his brother Andrew, James, John, Philip, Bartholomew, Matthew, Thomas, James son of Alphaeus, Simon who was called the Zealot, Judas son of James, and Judas Iscariot, who became a traitor.

Choosing friends is not a safe thing to do. It can be risky business. You might choose someone to be your friend who doesn't want to be your friend. You might choose a friend expecting to get a lot out of the relationship and discover that you have picked someone who drains you far more than energizes you. Friends can help, but friends can also hurt. There is always a risk that goes with friendship. But Jesus was ready and willing to take that risk, and so he selected a dozen friends.

There is nothing magical about the number twelve. It was the same number as the twelve sons of Jacob and the twelve territorial tribes of Israel. But, maybe it was twelve just because it was twelve. Whatever the reason and whatever the number, it was an unusually large number. Most of us would be grateful to have a few good friends. It is extremely rare to have a dozen close friends.

In some ways, they were not a very diverse lot. Most of them had much in common with Jesus. They were all Jews. They were similar in age. They were all men, although Jesus had a surprising number of women in his broader circle of friends. Eleven of the twelve were from Galilee, where Jesus grew up; one was from the province of Judea, where Jesus was born.

But when you start to inspect, you discover that there were differences among them. First on the list was Simon, who was a fisherman. He was a natural born leader. He was loud, in your face, and impulsive—very different from Jesus. But sometimes we choose friends who are not much like us.

Second on the list was Andrew. He was Simon's brother, but they were not much alike. Although Andrew partnered with his brother in the family fishing business on Galilee Lake, he actually had more of a spiritual bent to him. So he took a sabbatical from the fishing business and became a disciple of John the Baptizer, who later pointed him to Jesus. When Andrew met Jesus, one of the first things he did was introduce Simon to Jesus. He was a natural recruiter, a winsome and persuasive salesman, who recruited his own brother.

Third and fourth on the list were James and John. They also were brothers. They came from the upper middle class family of Zebedee with homes up north in Galilee and down south in Jerusalem. Their family was well connected and knew the political and religious leaders of their generation.

Philip was from Bethsaida, the same hometown as Simon and Andrew. It was a little town, and so Philip, Simon, and Andrew, being of similar age, would have known each other all their lives. Philip had a Greek name in a Hebrew culture. It makes you wonder why. It's a little like Mohammad at the synagogue or Sven in a Chinese restaurant.

Bartholomew is next. In the biographies of Jesus there are many different lists of his disciples, and often the lists are not complete—all twelve of the disciples are not always listed. But Bartholomew appears in every one of the lists. Yet, nothing else about him is ever said to identify him in the Bible. Other than his name, he is unknown in history. Some friends are kind of invisible but are always there, and Bartholomew, to his credit, always showed up.

Matthew was a tax collector. From all indications, he was a good and honorable man in a maligned profession. Because some tax collectors were greedy and cruel, he probably knew all the tax collector jokes and put up with the harassment that went along with his profession.

Thomas was a twin. He was known for his courage and for his analytical thoughtfulness. It makes you wonder why Jesus befriended two sets of brothers but chose only one of the twins.

James the son of Alphaeus had a mother named Mary. Beyond that, we know little about him. It seems strange that Jesus chose twelve close friends and two of them were named James. Maybe to avoid confusion, one was called James and the other Jimmy.

As the list progresses, there is another Simon to add to the confusion. This one is Simon the Zealot. In modern times that would be roughly equivalent to "Bill the Democrat" or "George the Republican." Zealots were members of a right-wing nationalistic political party. Many of them were into guerilla warfare. Some vowed to kill any Roman by any means at any time and carried daggers hidden in their clothes. You could say that he was Simon the Terrorist because that's pretty much what Zealots were. Terrorism is not new to our generation. How interesting that Jesus had one of the terrorists counted among his friends.

The last two both have the name Judas. Judas the son of James is a virtual unknown, although he did ask Jesus a question at the Last Supper. He was nicknamed Thaddeus, and, because of what happened with the other Judas, I think he preferred his nickname to being called Judas. Beyond that, we really don't know anything else about him.

Last on the list was Judas Iscariot. Of the twelve, he is the only one that was not from Jesus's home province of Galilee. We know quite a bit about the end of his life but not much about the beginning. What we do know is that out of the large crowds of those who could have been candidates to be among Jesus's dozen friends, Judas Iscariot was considered one of the best. Apparently, he was good with numbers and was considered to be trustworthy with money because he quickly became the treasurer of Jesus's group. He was the second Judas of the twelve.

There are some interesting—even curious—facts about this list of friends. Of the twelve, two were named Simon, two were named James, and two were named Judas. It's a bit like the boxer George Foreman who named all of his sons George. It must have been confusing. There seemed to be a shortage of names!

Several were given nicknames by Jesus. Simon he called Peter. (In English that would be Rocky!) James and John were The Sons of Thunder. Thomas was The Twin. Judas the son of James was called Thaddeus. Matthew was nicknamed Levi. James the son of Alphaeus was James the Younger/The Lesser (probably because he was smaller in size or younger in age—it was like being called Junior all your life!). Nathaniel was another nickname for one of the twelve, but we are not exactly sure which one.

Peter, Andrew, James, and John were all fishermen. Eleven of these twelve died violent deaths. James died by the sword in 44 CE under the rule of King Herod Agrippa. Judas Iscariot committed suicide. Peter was crucified. Of the dozen, only one died of old age and natural causes, and that was John.

Some became famous—so famous, in fact, that there are many men today who are named after them. Others we know little more than their names. Some were related. Of the twelve, three became part of an inner circle that was closer to Jesus than the other nine. They were Peter, James, and John. And of the three in the inner circle, there was one who was Jesus's best friend, and that was John.

These twelve became Jesus's delight. For more than three years, they walked and talked together, lived and ate together, took on critics, and basked together in the praise of large crowds. They climbed mountains, sailed stormy waters, shopped markets, studied the Bible, prayed, argued, laughed, cried, and shared their lives. They were friends.

When present-day soldiers are brought home from war because of injury or personal circumstances, they often insist on going back. The top reason isn't usually career or patriotism but friends. When people intensely share life together, they forge a bond that links their souls. That's the way it was with Jesus and his friends.

Picture the smile on Jesus's face when Peter jumped out of his boat and walked on the water to come to him. Imagine his emotions when these men pledged to give up anything to be with him. Think how pleased he must have been when they said they would rather die than abandon him. See his excitement when they said, *"Teach us to pray,"* and his delight when they memorized his words, *"Our Father in heaven, hallowed be your name."* Grasp the significance when his own family claimed that Jesus was out of his mind, but his twelve friends stood up for him and stuck by him. They were closer to him and better friends to him than his own family.

If you have some very good friends, you know the delight these disciples were to Jesus. But if you have very good friends, you also know that disappointment is often a part of friendship. Frankly, it was sometimes a two-way disappointment because Jesus disappointed these friends. They wanted Jesus to use his supernatural powers to conquer the Roman army, and Jesus disappointed them by saying, *"Blessed are the peacemakers."* They wanted him to call down fire from heaven on unbelieving villages, and Jesus refused. James and John asked for positions of prominence in Jesus's kingdom, and he turned them down. As much as they loved and admired Jesus, they were often disappointed with him. I think that must have weighed heavily on Jesus's heart. It is not easy to knowingly disappoint those you love the most.

But they also disappointed Jesus. He taught them intensely about humility, and they had outbursts of pride. Jesus gave special trust to Judas Iscariot— all of his money! But Judas betrayed him for an additional thirty silver coins. He asked them to pray for him when he was suffering, and they fell asleep. He really needed them to stand by him when he was arrested, but only two showed up for his trials, and one of them denied him three times. At his crucifixion, only John showed up to give him support when he was dying.

We all know what it is like to disappoint others, and we all know what it is like to be disappointed. But we don't all know what it is like to forgive and to be forgiven. Jesus was not going to allow these disappointments to fracture their friendships and end their relationships. If anything, he was going to use these disappointments to strengthen their relationships and make them lasting. He wanted them to be his friends for more than three years.

Some of the last recorded words Jesus said to these friends are found in Matthew 28:20: *"Surely I am with you always."* Of all the words to end his biography of Jesus, why did Matthew choose these? Because he knew their friendship was not over. Three years of friendship were not enough. They were friends forever. These words were written after Jesus returned to heaven. Matthew couldn't see him and touch him as he did during those first years together, but their friendship was stronger than ever before. Not even the distance between heaven and earth could diminish their relationship.

Perhaps we can understand why Matthew recorded these departing words of Jesus, but why did Jesus say them? It wasn't just for Matthew's sake (or for the two Simons, Andrew, James, John, Philip, Bartholomew, Thomas, Thaddeus or Nathaniel). It was also for Jesus' sake. He wanted them to continue to be his friends. He loved them. He wanted to spend eternity with them. He wanted to talk and laugh and reminisce and just hang out.

He didn't want their friendship ever to end. He wanted to be with them always. He wanted them to be his friends forever.

I told you our family moved to a town of 5000 when I was in seventh grade. I can still remember what it was like to walk to school alone. It wasn't very far, maybe 10 minutes, but it seemed like a very long way. I went home for lunch and then back to school in the afternoon. It was lonely. It was hard. And then one day, Dave and Judy invited me to walk with them. They lived in the same direction. They wanted to be my friends. It made all the difference.

Well, listen to this. Jesus wants to be our Friend. He doesn't want us to walk alone. But it's not just that he wants us to be with him; it's that he wants to be with us! You may be stunned by the words of Jesus recorded in John 15:13–16:

> *"Greater love has no one than this, to lay down one's life for one's friends. You are my friends if you do what I command . . . I have called you friends, for everything that I learned from my Father I have made known to you. You did not choose me, but I chose you."*

Jesus wants to make friends with you and me. He wants to add our names to the list. It's no longer just twelve. Now it's Peter and Paul; Andrew and Angie; James and John; Nathaniel and Naomi; Philip and Patty; Mary and Martha; Larry and Leith, and your name, too. Count yourself as a friend of Jesus Christ.

Worship Through Giving

"Be the Centre" by Michael Frye (© 1999 Vineyard songs [UK, Eire])

Key Lyrics: "Jesus, be the centre . . . be my source, be my light . . . Jesus"

Resource: Listening CD—*Hungry,* by Vineyard Music (2001, Vineyard Music). Listening CD—*Song Discovery Volume 46* (available at www.songdiscovery.com). Printed music at www.songdiscovery.com.

This song reflects the nature of intimacy with Christ. It is simple enough that the congregation could be asked to join in on the last chorus.

Worship Through Music

"You Surround Me" by Karen Padgett, Daphne Rademaker and Brian Doerksen (© 2002 Integrity's Hosanna!)

Key Lyrics: "I'll stay with you forever . . . arm and arm we'll walk together . . . you will never let me go"

Resource: Listening CD—*You Shine,* by Brian Doerksen (2002, Sony)

"King of Love" by Evan Cooper (© 2003 Parachute Music)

Key Lyrics: "Here I stand before you, Lord . . . I bare my soul . . . this gift for you . . . your grace that caused my soul to cry . . . tears that long for you"

Resource: Listening CD—*Glorious,* by Parachute Band (2003, Worship Extreme), available at http://worshipresources.parachutemusic.com.

FaithStory

One effective method of discipleship is the unique commitment of two people to a one-on-one spiritual growth relationship. The telling of this kind of real discipleship experience would encourage worshipers to consider deeper spiritual relationships in their own lives.

Worship Through Music

"Salt and Light" by Jan and John L'Ecuyer (© 2002 Integrity's Hosanna Music)

Key Lyrics: "You make me want to be like you . . . your holiness I will pursue . . . I want the heart of Jesus"

Resource: Listening CD—*Wash Over Me,* by Jami Smith (2002, Action Music)

Benediction

Christians one and all: May Jesus always be your best friend and may you always be a faithful friend and follower of Jesus Christ. Amen.

TRADITIONAL WORSHIP MUSIC OPTIONS:

Call to Worship Choir Anthem

"All Glory Be To God" by Young (© 1963 Galaxy Music Corp.)

Key Lyrics: "All glory be to God"

Feature Choir Anthem

"What a Friend We Have In Jesus" by Scriven/Arr. D. Hoehl (Public domain)

Key Lyrics: "Can we find a friend so faithful . . . who will all our sorrows share"

Hymn Options

"A Mighty Fortress Is Our God" words and music by Martin Luther, tr. Frederick Hedge (Public domain)

> Key Lyrics: "And though this world, with devils filled should threaten to undo us we will not fear, for God hath willed his truth to triumph through us"

"Praise My Soul the King of Heaven" words by Henry F. Lyte, music by John Goss (Public domain)

> Key Lyrics: "Father-like, he tends and spares us...all our hopes and fears he knows...in his hands he gently bears us...rescues us from all our foes"

"Sing Praise to the Father" by Clarkson/Doane Words (© 1966 Hope Publishing Co.)

> Key Lyrics: "Sing praise to the Savior...redeemer and Friend...for grace past all telling...for love without end"

"O Come to Me the Master Said" by Words: Dudley-Smith (© 1988 Hope Publishing Co.) Music: Adapt. Vaughan Williams (© Oxford University)

> Key Lyrics: "O come to me, the Master said...my Father knows your need...and I shall be, the Master said...your bread of life indeed"

"Jesus Is All the World to Me" words and music by Will L. Thompson (Public domain)

> Key Lyrics: "Jesus is all the world to me...my life, my joy, my all...he is my strength from day to day...without him I would fall"

"Our Great Savior" by Chapman/Prichard (Public domain)

> Key Lyrics: "Jesus! What a Friend for sinners...Jesus! Lover of my soul"

Service
4

Prayer That Does What Prayer Is Supposed To Do

THEME

Prayer

BIBLE PASSAGES

Mark 6:30–46

The apostles gathered around Jesus and reported to him all they had done and taught. Then, because so many people were coming and going that they did not even have a chance to eat, he said to them, "Come with me by yourselves to a quiet place and get some rest." So they went away by themselves in a boat to a solitary place. But many who saw them leaving recognized them and ran on foot from all the towns and got there ahead of them. When Jesus landed and saw a large crowd, he had compassion on them, because they were like sheep without a shepherd. So he began teaching them many things. By this time it was late in the day, so his disciples came to him. "This is a remote place," they said, "and it's already very late. Send the people away so they can go to the surrounding countryside and villages and buy themselves something to eat." But he answered, "You give them something to eat." They said to him, "That would take almost a year's wages! Are we to go and spend that much on bread and give it to them to eat?" "How many loaves do you have?" he asked. "Go and see." When they found out, they said, "Five—and two fish." Then Jesus directed them to have all the people sit down in groups on the green grass. So they sat down in groups of hundreds and fifties. Taking the five loaves and the two fish and looking up to heaven, he gave thanks and broke the loaves. Then he gave them to his disciples to set before the people. He also divided the two fish among them all. They all ate and were satisfied, and the disciples picked up twelve basketfuls of broken pieces of bread and fish. The number of the men who had eaten was five thousand. Immediately Jesus made his disciples get into the boat and go on ahead of him to Bethsaida, while he dismissed the crowd. After leaving them, he went up on a mountainside to pray.

SUMMARY

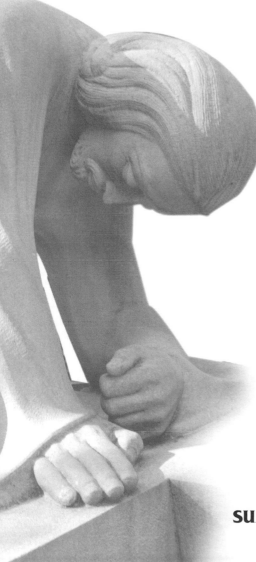

Prayer permeated the life of Jesus. He prayed before choosing his disciples. He left crowds and friends to pray alone. He told his followers to pray, and he showed them how to pray. He prayed before he was crucified, while he was being crucified, and after his resurrection. As Christians, we follow the principles and patterns of prayer set for us by Jesus.

SERVICE IMAGE

The DVD features a graphic image suitable for use during the "Prayer That Does What Prayer Is Supposed to Do" service. This suggested worship background shows a stained glass window with Jesus looking up toward the sky. This worship background appears on the *Abingdon Worship Photos, vol 3: Projection Images for Lent and Easter,* by Jim and Mary Whitmer (2003, Abingdon).

VIDEO

The DVD also features a video clip suitable for use during the "Prayer That Does What Prayer is Supposed to Do" service. This suggested video may be used at any point during the service.

CONTEMPORARY WORSHIP SEQUENCE:

Prelude

"Rise Up and Praise Him" by Paul Baloche and Gary Sadler (© 1996 Integrity's Hosanna! Music)

Key Lyrics: "worship the holy One with all your heart, with all your strength, with all your might"

Resource: Listening CD—i*WORSHIP, vol 2* (Integrity). Video—iWORSHIP DVD, vol E at www.integritymusic.com. Printed music at www.praisecharts.com

This song calls us to worship God with everything that we have! This song can be used in a number of ways: as a solo or with a group, with instruments or with tracks, and with lyrics projected over the video image or without.

Worship Through Music

"All Things Are Possible" by Darlene Zschech (© 1997, Hillsongs Australia)

Key Lyrics: "for in the power of your name all things are possible"

Resource: Listening CD—*All Things are Possible: Live Worship from Hillsongs Australia,* by Darlene Zschech (1997, Hillsongs Music). Printed music at www.praisecharts.com.

"Sing for Joy" by Lamont Heibert (© 1996, Integrity's Hosanna! Music)

Key Lyrics: "If we call to him, he will answer us; if we run to him, he will run to us"

Resource: Listening CD—*Vertical Momentum* (2004, Sony). Printed music at www.praisecharts.com.

Welcome

Following the theme of prayer, the welcome should include an invitation to experience the prayer ministries of the church. One idea would be to organize a Lenten noontime prayer service through the season of Lent with a different focus each week.

Worship Through Teaching

PRAYER THAT DOES WHAT PRAYER IS SUPPOSED TO DO
Matthew 6:7–13; Hebrews 10:5–7; Mark 6:30–52; John 17:1–26; Matthew 26:36–46

His disciples came to Jesus one day and said, "Jesus, teach us how to pray." Jesus told them to say:

Our Father in heaven, hallowed be your name, your kingdom come, your will be done, on earth as it is in heaven. Give us today our daily bread. And forgive us our debts as we also have forgiven our debtors. And lead us not into temptation, but deliver us from the evil one. (Matthew 6:7–13)

It was a very good answer. It was a very good example and a very good prayer. But what we call the Lord's Prayer was not the only lesson Jesus had in his school of prayer. Some of us learn better by looking than by listening. Some of us want more to our prayer life than the repetition of one very good prayer. We want prayers that do what prayers are supposed to do—connect us to God. So let's shadow Jesus. Let's follow him and eavesdrop on Jesus to see what we can learn about the way he prayed.

Interestingly, the first recorded prayer of Jesus in the New Testament is one you might never have guessed. It was prayed before he was born, even before he was named Jesus. That prayer is recorded in Hebrews 10:5–7:

Therefore, when Christ came into the world, he said: "Sacrifice and offering you did not desire, but a body you prepared for me; with burnt offerings and sin offerings you were not pleased. Then I said, 'Here I am—it is written about me in the scroll—I have come to do your will, my God.'"

Apparently, this was part of the farewell speech when the Son of God left heaven to come to earth. God the Father didn't want any more animal sacrifices to atone for human sin. He wanted to fix the relationship between humans and him once and for all. He loved the world so much that he decided to send his one and only Son. The Son of God, not yet called Jesus, said, "Yes! Here I am . . . I have come to do your will, my God."

Jesus's first recorded prayer was not asking but answering. It was not about getting but about giving. It was not about what he wanted but about what God wanted. This was the theme of Jesus's prayer life from before the beginning in the manger to the cross. He was always ready to do the will of his Father.

Let's fast-forward thirty-one years to one of the most successful days of Jesus's life. We can tell a lot about people by the way they handle success. Strangely, there seem to be more people who can handle failure well than those who can handle success well. Comparatively speaking, it is not the difficulties of life that can take us down but rather the great successes of life. Watch the actor who wins an Oscar. Watch the super athlete who scores a touchdown or wins the Super Bowl. Watch the politician who wins the office. Watch what happens when a neighbor or a relative inherits a fortune or wins the lottery. Watch the guy who gets the girl or the salesperson who sells the most. Watch Jesus celebrating success. We are told in Mark 6:30–46:

> *The apostles gathered around Jesus and reported to him all they had done and taught. Then, because so many people were coming and going that they did not even have a chance to eat, he said to them, "Come with me by yourselves to a quiet place and get some rest." So they went away by themselves in a boat to a solitary place. But many who saw them leaving recognized them and ran on foot from all the towns and got there ahead of them. When Jesus landed and saw a large crowd, he had compassion on them, because they were like sheep without a shepherd. So he began teaching them many things. By this time it was late in the day, so his disciples came to him. "This is a remote place," they said, "and it's already very late. Send the people away so they can go to the surrounding countryside and villages and buy themselves something to eat." But he answered, "You give them something to eat." They said to him, "That would take almost a year's wages! Are we to go and spend that much on bread and give it to them to eat?" "How many loaves do you have?" he asked. "Go and see." When they found out, they said, "Five—and two fish." Then Jesus directed them to have all the people sit down in groups on the green grass. So they sat down in groups of hundreds and fifties. Taking the five loaves and the two fish and looking up to heaven, he gave thanks and broke the loaves. Then he gave them to his disciples to set before the people. He also divided the two fish among them all. They all ate and were satisfied, and the disciples picked up twelve basketfuls of broken pieces of bread and fish. The number of the men who had eaten was five thousand. Immediately Jesus made his disciples get into the boat and go on ahead of him to Bethsaida, while he dismissed the crowd. After leaving them, he went up on a mountainside to pray.*

Jesus had performed one of the greatest miracles in all of history. He manipulated the forces of nature. He brought the powers of heaven down to earth. He satisfied the hunger of thousands of people. He became the center of attention and the celebrity of his generation. And how did he celebrate his success? *"He went up on a mountainside to pray."*

Please don't misunderstand. It wasn't that he didn't enjoy the praise of the people. It wasn't that he didn't like the party. It's just that God was the most important person in his life and when any of us experience our greatest success, we want to share that success with the person that is most important to us.

Put yourself in Jesus' sandals. When you have your best day—a promotion at work, your wedding day, the birth of your baby, the day you win the championship, the day your dreams come true—at the end of that day, sneak off to tell God all that has happened. Sneak off to pray.

Good days and difficult days sometimes come on the same day. Just when it seems life can't get any better, things can suddenly become frightening and difficult. Life is like that—a strange blend of the best and the worst, of victory and defeat, of bitter and sweet. For Jesus, the same prayer that celebrated success on the mountainside prepared him for the storm on the water. Mark 6:47–52 continues:

> *When evening came, the boat was in the middle of the lake, and he was alone on land. He saw the disciples straining at the oars, because the wind was against them. Shortly before dawn he went out to them, walking on the lake. He was about to pass by them, but when they saw him walking on the lake, they thought he was a ghost. They cried out, because they all saw him and were terrified. Immediately he spoke to them and said, "Take courage! It is I. Don't be afraid." Then he climbed into the boat with them, and the wind died down. They were completely amazed, for they had not understood about the loaves; their hearts were hardened.*

It was on Galilee Lake that this happened. While not a big lake—it's only about seven miles across—it is a deep lake surrounded by mountains, and storms come up quickly. I know. I was once caught in a storm out on Galilee Lake. It was scary! A group of us had rented a thirty foot fishing boat to go from one side of the lake to the other. It had a main deck and a set of stairs like a ladder that went up to an observation level. The day was clear and the water was calm as we left the dock, and most of the passengers went to the upper level for a better view. We were perhaps three-quarters of the way across the lake when, from nowhere, the winds whipped up and the small craft started to heave from side to side. We were top-heavy from all the people upstairs. The captain yelled for them to come down, but they were holding on with all their strength to avoid being thrown overboard. No way were they going to climb down. I was on the lower deck enjoying the excitement until I looked in the captain's eyes and saw panic. He had lived his entire life on this lake, and he was truly scared.

That's how it was for Jesus's friends that night on Galilee Lake. These were veteran sailors, but the storm was fierce and frightening, and their lives were at risk. They needed help. So Jesus stepped off the shore and onto the lake. He walked on the water to their boat. Now, if they were scared before, they were really scared when they saw what they thought was a ghost coming their way. When Jesus stepped into their boat the winds subsided and the waves became calm. Everything was safe. The storm was past.

How did he do that? What about the laws of physics? Through the years there have been an abundance of explanations given but no definitive answers. Let me offer you a super-physics explanation. This was the second major miracle in less than 24 hours. It was an act of God. It was the result of prayer.

Did Jesus know that the storm was coming? Probably not. Could he have walked on the water if he had not prayed? We are never told. But the principle here is important: Jesus prayed before the storm so that when the storm came he would be ready. Sometimes prayer is celebrating the successes. More often prayer is preparing us for the unknown-but-sure-to-come storms of life. Blessed are those who are prayed up before the storms come.

The longest recorded prayer of Jesus is reported in John 17:1–26. Sometimes it is called the "High Priestly Prayer." It was spoken in private, so the only way we know what was said is that Jesus told us.

Because the prayer is so long, we won't take the time to read it all here, but I want to tell you some things about it. First of all, Jesus kept his eyes open. We often close our eyes to minimize the distractions around us, but Jesus prayed wide-eyed and looking up toward the face of God. It was the typical Jewish stance.

Also, Jesus prayed for himself, for his disciples and for us. For himself he prayed, *"Father the hour has come"* [because he was nearing his death]. *"And now, Father, glorify me in your presence with the glory I had with you before the world began."*

Then he prayed for his disciples, *"Holy Father, protect them by the power of your name, the name you gave me, so that they may be one as we are one."* He was concerned about their safety after he died.

And then he prayed for us, *"My prayer is not for [my disciples] alone. I pray also for those who will believe in me through their message, that all of them may be one, Father, just as you are in me and I am in you."* How stunning to think that

Jesus, on his way to the cross, took time to stop and pray one of his longest prayers—and he had you and me in mind in that prayer! It is equally amazing that Jesus is still praying for us every day, including today.

The third point I would like to make is that Jesus's prayer can be hard to understand. It's not that the prayer is confusing, but it is personal and passionate. Jesus is simply talking things through with his Father, from his heart. That's what prayer was for Jesus. And that's what prayer is for many of us, as well. When we pray, we pour out our thoughts and feelings in words that others may not easily understand and might even find boring. But God is the best listener in the universe. In many ways, that is the heart of prayer—not so much about asking as it is just talking things through with the God who listens and cares.

Later that same week Jesus knew he had only hours left to live and he was overwhelmed. He thought about dying. He thought about the pain of crucifixion. He thought about having the sins of the world dumped on him. As a result, he was depressed.

Have you ever felt so totally down that you thought you might die? Have you ever been so discouraged you felt you couldn't face tomorrow? Have you ever felt totally overwhelmed? That's how Jesus felt the night before he died. Matthew 26:36–44 records Jesus's experience:

> *Then Jesus went with his disciples to a place called Gethsemane, and he said to them, "Sit here while I go over there and pray." He took Peter and the two sons of Zebedee along with him, and he began to be sorrowful and troubled. Then he said to them, "My soul is overwhelmed with sorrow to the point of death. Stay here and keep watch with me." Going a little farther, he fell with his face to the ground and prayed, "My Father, if it is possible, may this cup be taken from me. Yet not as I will, but as you will." Then he returned to his disciples and found them sleeping. "Couldn't you men keep watch with me for one hour?" he asked Peter. "Watch and pray so that you will not fall into temptation. The spirit is willing, but the flesh is weak." He went away a second time and prayed. "My Father, if it is not possible for this cup to be taken away unless I drink it, may your will be done." When he came back, he again found them sleeping, because their eyes were heavy. So he left them and went away once more and prayed the third time, saying the same thing.*

What did Jesus do when the weight of the world was crushing him? He prayed . . . and prayed . . . and prayed. Not standing with his eyes looking up to heaven but face-down on the ground. Desperate. Troubled. He poured his heart out to God for help and hope.

And God answered his prayer, but not in the way he asked. God has different ways of answering prayers. Sometimes it is exactly as we request; other times it is very different. God did not remove the horrors that Jesus faced; instead he took his beloved Son through those horrors to the other side.

Our last portrait of Jesus in prayer is not a pretty sight. He has been severely beaten, crucified, and abandoned by most of his friends. It was painful to see him then, and it is painful to picture him now. He felt forsaken by God and desperately alone, yet he prayed to his last breath. Luke 23:46 tells us, "Jesus called out with a loud voice, '*Father, into your hands I commit my spirit.' When he had said this, he breathed his last.*" Prayer was so woven into who Jesus was that he never stopped.

I don't pretend to understand what was going through his mind. Earlier he had said, *"My God, my God, why have you forsaken me?"* (Matthew 27:46). But I do know that his throat was parched and that he was in excruciating pain. If ever there was a moment when someone felt completely abandoned and alone, this was it. If there ever was a time you wouldn't pray, this was the time. But connection with God was so central to his life that he stayed connected to the last second of his life.

Did Jesus know at that moment that he would rise again from the dead? Intellectually, yes. He had predicted that he would come back to life again after three days. But when we are in pain and alone, our hearts don't always keep up with our heads. We don't always feel what we know. As Jesus was dying, he did to the last what he had done from the first. He committed himself to God the Father in prayer, even though his feelings must have been struggling to keep up with his faith.

All of this is not meant to be a lesson in prayer. It is meant to be an encounter with Jesus. When we experience Jesus, we want to be like him. Who he is drives us to him and what he did. As Christians we are drawn to pray as he prayed—when leaving home, when celebrating success, when walking into a raging storm, when talking about life, when feeling overwhelmed, and even right up to our very last breath. You see, Jesus has taught us a whole lot more than the words of the Lord's Prayer. He actually showed us how to pray.

Worship Through Drama

(Please view the drama on the resource DVD. The drama is available as both a performance and a script.)

THE SECRET SOURCE
(Written by Shelly Barsuhn)

Characters/cast: MOM
DAD
DANIELLE, 8–10 years old
CALEB, 8–10 years old

Props: Notebook
      Pencil
      Bench
      Chair

(DANIELLE enters. She sits down on the bench and bows her head. MOM and DAD enter and stand apart, watching her.)

MOM: Look at her. When she was a baby, I rocked her and rocked her and couldn't stop gazing at her. I've been doing it again, lately. Staring at her—as if I'll never get enough.

DAD: She a wonderful girl.

MOM: How can she be so sick?

DAD: Remember. We don't know, for sure, how serious it is.

(MOM is suddenly distraught.)

DAD: *(softly)* I wish you could just let go of the worry for a moment. Take a break. Get some distance. You're under a lot of stress.

MOM: *(fiercely)* How can you even say that to me? Distance! After everything we've been through with her lately!

DAD: Just for a moment.

MOM: Tell me how! Tell me how to get distance when my daughter is ill!

(MOM and DAD look at each other, then embrace.)

DAD: Sometimes it seems as if she's the strong one.

(CALEB enters, carrying notebook and pencil. He approaches DANIELLE.)

CALEB: *(to DANIELLE)* What's wrong with you? You looked sad. Your head was down.

DANIELLE: I was praying.

CALEB: How come?

(DANIELLE shrugs.)

DANIELLE: Just because. It's what I do.

CALEB: I pray at bedtime. When my mom makes me.

DANIELLE: I pray a lot. Especially when I'm upset about stuff.

CALEB:	Don't people hear you?
DANIELLE:	Not if I don't pray out loud, crazy. Don't you know God can hear you even if you don't say the words? You can just think them up here *(pointing to her temple).*
CALEB:	I always say my prayers out loud. Just in case.
MOM:	They look serious. What are they talking about?
DAD:	Kid stuff. Chocolate chip cookies. Game Boys. Disneyland.
DANIELLE:	So did you hear?
CALEB:	Hear what?
DANIELLE:	I'm sick.
CALEB:	*(backing away)* You are? What do you have?
DANIELLE:	Nothing that you can catch.
CALEB:	*(approaching again)* You don't look sick.
DANIELLE:	It's inside.
CALEB:	Do you have to get a shot or something?
DANIELLE:	I don't know. We're talking to a lot of doctors.
	(CALEB absorbs this. After a pause . . .)
CALEB:	Is that why you were praying?
DANIELLE:	Uh huh.
DAD:	Kids are resilient. She's not as worried as we are.
MOM:	But Danielle's always been unusual that way. She has inner strength. Where does she get that?
DAD:	My side of the family?
MOM:	Right. Like you're not quaking on the inside, too.
	(CALEB starts writing on the notebook.)
DANIELLE:	What are you doing?
CALEB:	Writing you a get-well note. "Get . . . Well . . . " You have a long name. "D-A-N-"

DANIELLE: You could pray for me, too. Not just when you go to bed. Whenever it pops into your head. I'm going to need more prayers.

CALEB: What should I say?

DANIELLE: Well . . . I'd like to get better. Ask God for that. And make the doctors not get any crazy ideas about giving me shots.

CALEB: Got it.

(CALEB starts to exit.)

DANIELLE: Hey. Where are you going?

CALEB: Home. To pray.

DANIELLE: *(exasperated)* I told you. You can pray anywhere. Just stand there and do it.

CALEB: Right now? Here?

DANIELLE: Yes!

(CALEB bows his head. He opens his eyes and sees DANIELLE watching him. He turns abruptly to face away from her.)

MOM: Do you think Danielle will tell him? I dread having to tell people. *(sudden idea)* Could we just keep it quiet? It could be a secret until after the treatments are over and we know—

DAD: We can't do this by ourselves!

MOM: How can anybody help? We are alone!

DANIELLE: You done?

CALEB: Yes.

DANIELLE: Did you pray what I told you?

CALEB: Yes.

DANIELLE: *(breathing a sigh of relief)* Oh, thank you. That feels good. Prayer is powerful, you know.

CALEB: *(Looking up and seeing DANIELLE'S parents watching them.)* Maybe you should tell your parents. They look worried.

DANIELLE: *(looking up)* Do you think they'd understand?

CALEB: I don't know. It's worth a shot.

DANIELLE: Right. Maybe if they hear it from me.

(Freeze—DANIELLE and CALEB looking toward MOM and DAD.)

(All exit.)

Worship Through Giving

"Where Two or Three" by Graham Kendrick (© 1996 Make Way Music)

Key Lyrics: "Where two or three of you gather in my name, I am there . . . I am there with you"

Resource: Listening CD—*No More Walls* (1997, Alliance). CD and sheet music available at http://www.fierceshop.com/. More information at http://www.grahamkendrick.co.uk.

This song is a direct meditation on the act of prayer as prescribed by Jesus. It is an intimate worship song that is simple enough for the congregation to join singing on the last chorus.

Worship Through Music

"Heavenly Father" by Cheri Keaggy (© 1996 Sparrow Song)

Key Lyrics: "Father, heavenly Father, have I told you I love you today, have I told you I need you"

Resource: Listening CD—*My Faith Will Stay*, by Cheri Keaggy (1996, Sparrow/Emd).

Recite the Lord's Prayer during the musical introduction of the next song

"The Lord's Prayer" by Matt Shepardson (© 1999 Ever Devoted Music.)

Key Lyrics: "Father in heaven . . . all praise be to your name . . . Your kingdom come, your will be done on earth as it is in heaven" (This is a modern, upbeat arrangement of the Lord's Prayer.)

Resource: Lyrics, video, demo track, rehearsal track, and printed music at www.willowcreek.com/resources/music.asp (Search for "The Lord's Prayer" or use the following url—http://www.willowcreek.com/arrangement.asp?action=details&arrangementid=1140&sid=12).

FaithStory

Two options for the faith story are: 1) a person that came to faith in Jesus Christ as a result of a person or group of people praying for them, or 2) an individual that experienced personal change because of a prayer experience or discipline.

Worship Through Music

"Knocking On the Door of Heaven" by Matt Redman and Steve Cantellow (© 1996 Kingsway's Thankyou Music ASCAP)

Key Lyrics: "We will give ourselves no rest 'til your kingdom comes on earth . . . we've positioned watchmen on the walls . . . now our prayers will flow like tears for you've shared your heart with us . . . God of heaven, on our knees we fall"

Resource: Listening CD—*Passion: Live Worship from the 268 Generation* (1998, Passion Conferences), available at www.268store.com.

Benediction

Pray to Jesus. Pray like Jesus. And may all your prayers be answered by Jesus. Amen.

TRADITIONAL WORSHIP MUSIC OPTIONS:

Feature Choir Anthem

"The Lord's Prayer" by Malotte, Arr. Stickles (© 1959 G Schirmer)

Key Lyrics: "Our Father which art in heaven hallowed by thy name, thy kingdom come, thy will be done on earth as it is in heaven"

Hymn Options

"Holy God We Praise Your Name" by Attr. Ignaz Franz, tr. Clarence Walwoarth/ Katholisches Gesangbuch (Public domain)

Key Lyrics: "Lord of all, we bow before you . . . all on earth your scepter claim . . . all in heaven above adore you"

"Brethren We Have Met To Worship" words by George Atkins, music by William Moore (Public domain)

Key Lyrics: "Brethren, we have met to worship and adore the Lord our God . . . Will you pray with all your power while we try to preach the Word"

"Draw Me Nearer" words by Frances J. Crosby, music by William H. Doane (Public domain)

Key Lyrics: "I am thine, O Lord, I have heard thy voice and it told thy love to me but I long to rise in the arms of faith and be closer drawn to thee"

"Sweet Hour of Prayer" words by William Walford, music by William B. Bradbury (Public domain)

Key Lyrics: "Sweet hour of prayer . . . that calls me from a world of care and bids me at my Father's throne . . . make all my wants and wishes known"

"Lord Teach Us How to Pray Aright" by James Montgomery/Haweis, adapt Webbe, Jr. (Public domain)

Key Lyrics: "Lord, teach us how to pray aright with reverence and with fear . . . though weak and sinful in your sight we may, we must draw near"

Service 5

Experiencing Miracles

THEME

Supernatural power

BIBLE PASSAGES

Luke 19:37
When [Jesus] came near the place where the road goes down the Mount of Olives, the whole crowd of disciples began joyfully to praise God in loud voices for all the miracles they had seen.

SUMMARY

Miracles marked the ministry of Jesus. From changing water into wine at Cana to raising Lazarus from the dead at Bethany, Jesus repeatedly performed miracles to meet human need and persuade people to believe. During the week before Palm Sunday, the word spread through the pilgrims in Jerusalem about all Jesus did, and they thronged to him, shouting praises in loud voices because of the miracles they had seen. Jesus is still the miracle worker in our world and lives today.

SERVICE IMAGE

The DVD features a graphic image suitable for use during the "Experiencing Miracles" service. This suggested worship background shows a cross with beams of color bursting from the middle. This worship background appears on the *Abingdon Worship Photos, vol 3: Projection Images for Lent and Easter,* by Jim and Mary Whitmer (2003, Abingdon).

CONTEMPORARY SERVICE SEQUENCE:

Prelude

These two prelude options create an atmosphere of anticipation and belief in the power of God. Both songs feature the worship vocalists and band. The lyrics speak of the limitless power of God at work in the world and our lives.

Option #1

"Indescribable" by Laura Story and Jesse Reeves (© 2004 Worship-together.com)

Key Lyrics: "Indescribable, uncontainable, you placed the stars in the sky and you know them by name. You are amazing God…all powerful, untamable, awestruck we fall to our knees as we humbly proclaim: you are amazing God"

Resource: Listening CD—*Arriving,* by Chris Tomlin. Printed music at www.praisecharts.com.

Option #2

"All the Power You Need" by Russell Fragar (1996 Russell Fragar/ Hillsongs Australia)

Key Lyrics: "My God can never fail…he's been proved time and again… trust him and see he's got all the power you need"

Resource: Listening CD—*Shout to the Lord: The Platinum Collection* (2000, Sony). Printed music at www.integritymusic.com.

Worship Through Music and Creed

"God Is Great" by Marty Sampson (© 2001 Marty Sampson/Hillsong)

Key Lyrics: "All creation cries to you…worshiping in spirit and in truth …glory to the Faithful One…Jesus Christ, God's Son"

Resource: Listening CD—*You are My World: Live* (2001, Sony). Printed music at www.praisecharts.com and www.integritymusic.com.

"Awesome in This Place" by Ned Davies (© 1999 Ned Davies/Hillsongs)

Key Lyrics: "There is power here for miracles set the captives free make the broken whole"

Resource: Listening CD—*SongDiscovery, vol 24* (available at www.songdiscovery.com). Printed music at www.praisecharts.com and www.integritymusic.com.

The Apostles' Creed (Public domain) (Spoken)

I believe in God the Father Almighty,
  creator of heaven and earth.

I believe in Jesus Christ, his only Son, our Lord,
  who was conceived by the Holy Spirit,

born of the virgin Mary,
suffered under Pontius Pilate,
was crucified, died, and was buried;
he descended to the dead.
On the third day he rose again;
he ascended into heaven,
is seated at the right hand of the Father
and will come again to judge the living and the dead.

I believe in the Holy Spirit,
the holy catholic church,
the communion of saints,
the forgiveness of sins,
the resurrection of the body
and the life everlasting. Amen.

"I Stand In Awe" by Mark Altrogge (© 1988 by People of Destiny Music/Pleasant HillMusic)

Key Lyrics: "Who can grasp your infinite wisdom . . . who can fathom the depth of your love . . . you are beautiful beyond description . . . majesty enthroned above"

Resource: Listening CD—*I Stand in Awe: Worship Favorites from Sovereign Grace Music* (2002, Sovereign Grace Music). Listening CD—*Songs4Worship: Be Glorified* (2001, Time Life Records). Printed music at www.praisecharts.com and www.integritymusic.com.

Welcome

Worship Through Giving

"God" by Rebecca St. James and Tedd T (© 1996 Up in The Mix Music)

Key Lyrics: "He made the night . . . he made the day spread the earth upon the waters made the heavens and the rain . . . look at the sky . . . see its design . . . the very same creator is the one who gave us life . . . and what is man that He's mindful of us we're merely clay in His hands"

Resource: Listening CD—*God,* by Rebecca St. James (1996, Forefront/Emd).

One video possibility for this feature song is a collage of clips from any of the biographical films on the life of Jesus, a popular animation like *The Prince of Egypt,* and other various videos that feature miraculous works of God. Once edited into a continuous series of clips, it can be played while the worship team sings the song.

Worship Through Teaching

EXPERIENCING MIRACLES
Luke 19:37

Do you believe in miracles? The Louis Finkelstein Institute for Religious and Social Studies at New York's Jewish Theological Seminary sponsored a national survey in December 2004 questioning 1100 doctors about miracles. 74 percent of physicians believed that miracles occurred in the past, and 73 percent of physicians believe that miracles can occur today.

Then there is the broader audience of a poll conducted by Newsweek magazine. This poll revealed that 84 percent of Americans believe in divine miracles, 79 percent believe the miracles in the Bible, 48 percent say they have personally experienced miracles, 63 percent know people who have experienced a miracle, and 67 percent of Americans say they have prayed for a miracle.

Some of us are skeptical. Others of us easily believe. It is a worthwhile debate as to whether or not we ought to believe in miracles, but for now, we simply want to see for ourselves what Jesus did.

We are walking with Jesus during forty days before Easter, and next weekend is Palm Sunday, the anniversary of the day large crowds formed a parade to usher Jesus into Jerusalem. They waved palm branches, took off their coats to carpet the road, and shouted exorbitant praise to him. But do you know how it all got started? That is explained in Luke 19:37:

> *[Jesus] came near the place where the road goes down the Mount of Olives, the whole crowd of disciples began joyfully to praise God in loud voices for all the miracles they had seen.*

What was it like to experience the miracles of Jesus? It all began in a little village called Cana in the northern province of Galilee when Jesus attended a wedding reception that ran out of wine. When they asked for his help, he spoke a word and changed nearly 180 gallons of ordinary water into high quality wine. This was the first of Jesus's miracles, and it was a very impressive beginning. But it was not as personal as miracle number two.

A second miracle of Jesus came on a return visit to the same village. It is found in John 4:46–53:

> *Once more he visited Cana in Galilee, where he had turned the water into wine. And there was a certain royal official whose son lay sick at Capernaum. When this man heard that Jesus had arrived in Galilee from Judea, he went to him and begged him to come and heal his son, who was close to death. "Unless you people see miraculous signs and wonders," Jesus told him, "you will never believe." The royal official said, "Sir, come down before my child dies." "Go," Jesus*

replied, "your son will live." The man took Jesus at his word and departed. While he was still on the way, his servants met him with the news that his boy was living. When he inquired as to the time when his son got better, they said to him, "Yesterday, at one in the afternoon, the fever left him." Then the father realized that this was the exact time at which Jesus had said to him "Your son will live." So he and his whole household believed.

This man who came to Jesus was an official in the royal court of Herod Antipas. He was an aristocrat with position, power, and money—and a dying son. When your child is sick, celebrity status means very little. The disbelief of other people isn't important. This man was desperate. He knew he risked being absent at the very moment his son would die. But he had no other hope. He had traveled a full day's journey from Capernaum to Cana hoping for a miracle, so he begged Jesus to come and heal his boy before the child died.

Jesus never went. He spoke a word and the boy was healed. Jesus can do that, you know. He hears the pleas of parents with sick children and performs miracles—even from a distance.

When this desperate dad got the message that his son's fever had broken and he was well, and when he found out that it had occurred the exact moment that Jesus had spoken, he believed. He started out with relatively little faith, and his little faith grew large. He believed and everyone in his household believed as well. That's what happens when Jesus heals your child.

In John 5:1–9 we are told:

Some time later, Jesus went up to Jerusalem for one of the Jewish festivals. Now there is in Jerusalem near the Sheep Gate a pool, which in Aramaic is called Bethesda and which is surrounded by five covered colonnades. Here a great number of disabled people used to lie—the blind, the lame, the paralyzed. One who was there had been an invalid for thirty-eight years. When Jesus saw him lying there and learned that he had been in this condition for a long time, he asked him, "Do you want to get well?" "Sir," the invalid replied, "I have no one to help me into the pool when the water is stirred. While I am trying to get in, someone else goes down ahead of me." Then Jesus said to him, "Get up! Pick up your mat and walk." At once the man was cured; he picked up his mat and walked.

How does someone hold on to hope for thirty-eight years? We are not told how old he was, but thirty-eight years was greater than the life expectancy of his generation. He hung out at a healing shrine—they were common in the first century Roman world—where there were supposed to be magical or supernatural powers for healing available. He did this for almost forty years. When you are desperate enough, you will hang in for a long time.

But obviously it didn't work for this man. He was no better than he had been at the beginning.

This man didn't come to Jesus. He couldn't come to Jesus. He didn't ask Jesus for a miracle. In fact, he didn't even know who Jesus was. But Jesus came to him. Jesus asked him if he wanted a miracle. So, the miracles of Jesus were not limited to those who had fathers who would come and beg. They were not limited to those who were holy and good. Jesus sought out the sick. Jesus found the disabled. Jesus wanted to help the disabled man even more than the disabled man wanted to be helped.

Then there was the time with the demon in Matthew 9:32–33:

> *A man who was demon possessed and could not talk was brought to Jesus. And when the demon was driven out, the man who had been mute spoke. The crowd was amazed and said, "Nothing like this has ever been seen in Israel."*

Demons seem farfetched to a lot of people in present-day America. We would have sent this man to a speech therapist and assumed there was some medical or psychological explanation. But to most people in history and for the majority of people in the world today, demons are anything but farfetched. They are very real and powerful and frightening. In fact, probably a majority of people in our world today think it strange that we seek scientific solutions for clearly spiritual maladies.

Now, certainly not all physical problems are because of demonic activity. But some are. And apparently this one was. A demon had somehow gotten into this person so that he was unable to speak. All of his thoughts and expressions were trapped in his head and could not get out of his mouth. That meant that he could never pick up his own child and say, "I love you." He could never ask God to deliver him. But, fortunately, other people cared about him and brought him to Jesus, believing that Jesus could and would help him.

Interestingly, we are not told what Jesus said or did. The point here is that when the demon faced off with Jesus, the demon lost and Jesus won. This once speechless man spoke. He was free at last and could shout for joy.

I don't know whether or not you are impressed, but those who witnessed what happened were very impressed. They had never before seen or heard of such a thing. It was amazing. They said, "Nothing like this has ever been seen in Israel."

It was unprecedented. What Jesus was doing did not fit in any of the established categories. But it wasn't just for the Jews in Israel that Jesus performed his miracles. In Matthew 15:21–28 we read:

Jesus withdrew to the region of Tyre and Sidon. A Canaanite woman from that vicinity came to him, crying out, "Lord, Son of David, have mercy on me! My daughter is demon-possessed and suffering terribly." Jesus did not answer a word. So his disciples came to him and urged him, "Send her away, for she keeps crying out after us." He answered, "I was sent only to the lost sheep of Israel." The woman came and knelt before him, "Lord, help me!" she said. He replied, "It is not right to take the children's bread and toss it to their dogs." "Yes it is, Lord," she said, "Even the dogs eat the crumbs that fall from their master's table." Then Jesus said to her, "Woman, you have great faith! Your request is granted." And her daughter was healed from that very hour.

Jesus was a Jew in Gentile territory. Tyre and Sidon were pagan places. This was not an area where Jews typically lived or even visited. To describe the woman as a Canaanite bordered on a racial slur because many of the Jews hated the Canaanites. They were the ones who originally inhabited what for the descendents of Abraham was the Promised Land. There was continued Jewish animosity and racism toward these ancient people.

But spiritual and physical needs are not limited to people who believe in the God of the Bible. Pagans need miracles, too. This Canaanite mother was tortured by her daughter's chronic problems. Nothing had worked. Nothing had helped. Her daughter had a demon wrecking her life from the inside out. So this mother came to Jesus and pleaded for help. And Jesus did nothing. He didn't even answer her.

But she wouldn't quit. She was annoyingly persistent—following, begging, crying. In present-day terminology we might say she was stalking Jesus. Jesus's disciples asked Jesus to use his powers to get rid of her, to make her go away. When Jesus explained that his first calling was to the Jews, not the pagans, she fell on her knees and pleaded, "Lord, help me! Just let me have a crumb of a miracle for my daughter."

I don't know why Jesus was so reluctant to help her. I have never been able to explain why some people get miracles and others don't. But it seems obvious to me that Jesus was impressed by her persistence. She simply would not quit trying to get Jesus to heal her daughter.

Jesus finally said yes. He spoke the word and the daughter was set free from the demon. After all that waiting, she finally got her miracle. All it took was a word from Jesus.

Can you imagine how the mother felt? What must it have been like for the girl to finally be demon-free? I think if she were here today she would say, "Never give up trying to get a miracle from Jesus!"

All of Jesus's miracles were amazing, but none was more amazing than the one reported in John 11. It all started when Lazarus, a friend of Jesus, got sick one day. We all get sick, and most of us get better. But Lazarus didn't get better. He kept getting worse. When his two sisters realized that he was dying, they sent a message for Jesus to come as quickly as possible. But Jesus was too far away, and Lazarus died.

Instead of coming to his sick bed, Jesus came to his friend's wake. His sisters were glad Jesus came, but they confronted him for not coming in time. We read in John 11:21, "*'Lord,' Martha said to Jesus, 'if you had been here, my brother would not have died.'*"

What good is a miracle worker who shows up four days late? They could not help but be disappointed with Jesus. But the very day they all thought Jesus had failed them turned out to be the day he performed his greatest miracle of all. In John 11:43–44 we are told that Jesus stood by the cave where Lazarus was buried and "*Jesus called in a loud voice, 'Lazarus, come out!' The dead man came out, his hands and feet wrapped with strips of linen, and a cloth around his face.*"

Jesus raised a man from the dead! This dwarfs everything else: changing water to wine, chasing a demon out of a child, or enabling someone who couldn't speak to speak. This was the miracle of Jesus's miracles. If Jesus could do this, then he could do anything.

Jesus said to his friend Martha in John 11:25:

> *'I am the resurrection and the life. Anyone who believes in me will live, even though they die; and whoever lives by believing in me will never die. Do you believe this?' 'Yes, Lord,' she told him, 'I believe that you are the Messiah, the Son of God, who was to come into the world.'*

If you believe that Jesus raised a person from the dead, you can believe everything about Jesus. These were just some of Jesus's miracles. In John 20:30–31 we are told:

> *Jesus performed many other miraculous signs in the presence of his disciples, which are not recorded in this book. But these are written that you may believe that Jesus is the Messiah, the Son of God, and that by believing you may have life in his name.*"

It's no wonder they paraded him and praised him on Palm Sunday. Luke 19:37 tells us:

> *When [Jesus] came near the place where the road goes down the Mount of Olives, the whole crowd of disciples began joyfully to praise God in loud voices for all the miracles they had seen.*

I wonder what miracles of Jesus we will experience this week!

Worship Through Music

"In Need" by Ross King (© 1996 Ross King)

Key Lyrics: "In need of Christ, the perfect Lamb . . . my refuge strong . . . the great I am"

Resource: Listening CD—*To Make God Famous*, by Ross King (2002).

"This Kingdom" by Geoff Bullock (© 1995 Word Music, Inc./Maranatha! Music)

Key Lyrics: "Jesus redemption's sacrifice . . . now glorified, now justified . . . his kingdom come . . . For the majesty and power of this kingdom's King has come"

Resource: Listening CD—*Australia's Top 25 Praise Songs* (2001, Maranatha). Printed music at www.integritymusic.com.

FaithStory

Worship Through Music

"More Love, More Power" by Jude Del Hierro (© 1987 Mercy Publishing)

Key Lyrics: "More Love, more power, more of you in my life"

Resource: Listening CD—*WOW Worship: Yellow* (2003, Benson).

Originally written as a worship ballad, the *WOW Yellow* contemporary artist compilation recording features an updated arrangement of "More Love, More Power" that is both driving and a strong conclusion to a service about the miraculous power of God.

Benediction

May the supernatural power of Jesus Christ touch your life and result in great praise to God. Amen.

TRADITIONAL WORSHIP MUSIC OPTIONS:

Call to Worship Choir Anthem

"Beautiful Savior" by Anonymous, arr. Fettke (© 1978 Lillenas Pub. Co.)

Key Lyrics: "Beautiful Savior, Lord of the nations, Son of God and Son of Man"

Feature Choir Anthem

"What a Friend we Have In Jesus" words by Joseph M. Scriven, music by Charles C. Converse, arr. Dave Hoehl (Public domain)

Key Lyrics: "Can we find a friend so faithful . . . who will all our sorrows share"

Resource: For Dave Hoehl's custom arrangement of this public domain song, contact Dave Hoehl, Traditional Worship Director, Wooddale Church, 6630 Shady Oak Road, Eden Prairie, MN 55344.

Hymn Options

"A Mighty Fortress Is Our God" words and music by Martin Luther, tr. Frederick Hedge (Public domain)

Key Lyrics: "And though this world, with devils filled should threaten to undo us we will not fear, for God hath willed his truth to triumph through us"

"Praise the Lord Who Reigns Above" words by Charles Wesley (Public domain)

Key Lyrics: "Praise the Lord who reigns above . . . Praise him for his noble deeds . . . Praise him for his matchless power"

"God of Creation All Powerful" by E. Margaret Clarkson/Trad. Irish; harm: Hustad (Words © 1987 Hope Publishing Company. Music © 1974 Hope Publishing Company.)

Key Lyrics: "God of creation, all powerful, all wise . . . Lord of the universe rich with surprise . . . Maker, Sustainer, and Ruler of all . . . We are your children—you hear when we call"

"I Sing the Mighty Power of God" words by Isaac Watts (Public domain)

Key Lyrics: "I sing the mighty power of God that made the mountains rise . . . that spread the flowing seas abroad and built the lofty skies"

"We Will Extol You" by Psalm 145:1–10; para: J. Nichol Grieve/Genevan Psalter (© 1997 Lorenz Publishing Company)

Key Lyrics: "Your mighty acts with joy and fear relate"

Service 6

Going Through Suffering

THEME

Suffering

BIBLE PASSAGES

Several 'Passion of Jesus' Bible passages

Peter 2:23–25; Matthew 27:11–66; Mark 15; Luke 22:1–23:56; John 18–19

SUMMARY

Two important truths should be remembered through Holy Week: (1) Jesus suffered greatly, and (2) Jesus suffered for us. He bore our sins. This should cause both sadness and very great joy. We must never forget. We must take full advantage of all Jesus did for us.

SERVICE IMAGE

The DVD features a graphic image suitable for use during the "Going Through Suffering" service. This suggested worship background shows Jesus on the cross. This worship background appears on the Abingdon *Worship Photos, vol 3: Projection Images for Lent and Easter,* by Jim and Mary Whitmer (2003, Abingdon).

CONTEMPORARY SERVICE SEQUENCE (Palm Sunday)

Prelude

Part A: Video

Video clip from the movie *Jesus of Nazareth* (1977, Lions Gate Home Entertainment, director Franco Zeffirrelli) showing Jesus entering Jerusalem on a donkey.

Part B: Children's Choir Special

"Shout Hosanna!" Wright (© 1999 Choristers Guild)

Key Lyrics: "Can it be, is it he riding on the donkey . . . can it be, is it he, Jesus of Galilee"

Additional: Palm Sunday worship experiences frequently feature palm branches as a way to engage the congregation in the meaning of the service. Utilize the children's choir to wave palm branches as they enter the worship space. Also, have the children participate in leading the first songs of the worship service to provide integration and a learning opportunity for the children.

Worship Through Music

"Lord of Heaven" by Ashwood (© 1996 Out of the Door Music)

Key Lyrics: "Hosanna, blessed is he . . . let all the earth praise your name"

Resource: Church of the Open Door, 9060 Zanzibar Lane N., Maple Grove, Minnesota; (763) 416-5887.

"You Are My All in All" by Dennis Jernigan (© 1991 Shepherd's Heart Music, Inc.)

Key Lyrics: "Taking my sin, my cross, my shame rising again, I bless your name . . . you are my all in all"

Resource: Listening CD—*Girls of Grace* (2002, Word). Listening CD—*Giant Killer: A Heart Like David*, by Dennis Jernigan. Printed music at www.integritymusic.com.

Welcome

This worship service marks the beginning of Holy Week. To bring the congregation into the experience of Holy Week, it would be meaningful to lead a directed prayer on themes of gratitude, forgiveness, and dedication following the welcome. For example (this might need further explanation so people know what to do during the silent prayer responses):

Heavenly Father, the week we now enter is an opportunity to remember what you accomplished through Jesus Christ and his final journey to the cross. Even more, this week offers us a path to forgiveness and eternal life through Jesus Christ our Lord.

For Jesus, the week began with a marvelous entry to Jerusalem, grew in depth and emotion amid a Passover celebration with friends, but eventually plunged into darkness while suffering at the hands of enemies. You, Oh God, however, would not be denied your will and purpose for the redemption of humankind. So, in the greatest of all moments from the beginning of time until now, you accomplished a complete victory over sin and death in the resurrection event.

Gratitude
Jesus, meet us today as we celebrate your entrance into Jerusalem on a donkey. Knowing you as the humble king, we offer to you our gratitude for the journey that you took for our sake. (pause for silent prayers of gratitude)

Forgiveness
Heavenly Father, help us to embrace the meaning of Jesus Christ as the Passover Lamb, a necessary sacrifice for our sins. May we now offer our sins to you and ask that you cleanse our lives anew. (pause for silent prayers of forgiveness)

Dedication
Holy Spirit, ignite within us a spirit of gratitude and commitment to the cause of Jesus Christ in light of the Resurrection. We ask that the victory of Jesus Christ be our victory and the imitation of Jesus our life goal. To this end we dedicate our lives. (pause for silent prayers of dedication)

God, three in one, we give you this Holy Week as a week of transformation and full engagement in your salvation story. In the name of Jesus Christ our Lord, amen.

Worship Through Teaching

GOING THROUGH SUFFERING
Matthew 16:21–22; Matthew 27:28–30; Mark 15:34; 1 Peter 2:24;
2 Corinthians 5:21

Jesus knew what was coming. Long before the week of his death, he told his followers what to expect. It started on a day recorded in Matthew 16:21–22:

> *Jesus begin to explain to his disciples that he must go to Jerusalem and suffer many things at the hands of the elders, the chief priests and the teachers of the law, and that he must be killed and on the third day be raised to life. Peter took him aside and began to rebuke him. "Never, Lord!" he said. "This shall never happen to you!"*

Jesus's teachings were tremendous. His miracles were marvelous. But at the very center of what Jesus was all about was his suffering. It's not everything that Jesus was about, but it is extremely important. You cannot begin to understand Jesus without understanding his suffering. And the suffering of Jesus was not limited to the physical horrors of scourging and crucifixion. It started with his humiliation.

The praise on Palm Sunday was the "last straw" for the religious leaders of Jerusalem who had come to hate this Jesus of Nazareth. Matthew 27:28–30 records the details:

> *They stripped him and put a scarlet robe on him, and then twisted together a crown of thorns and set it on his head. They put a staff in his right hand as a scepter. Then they knelt in front of him and mocked him. "Hail, king of the Jews!" they said. They spit on him, and took the staff and struck him on the head again and again.*

Suffering from humiliation can be as bad as or even worse than physical pain. It is one of the strategies of terrorists and counter-terrorists. We all know stories of prisoners being stripped naked for public view, putting victims in embarrassing situations and laughing at them, mocking someone at his or her greatest vulnerability. It is all about disrespect and the abuse of power. It is putting someone down in the worst of ways.

To some extent, we have all been humiliated at one time or another. It may have been by a bully at school, by a parent who behaved badly, by a criminal who assaulted, by a spouse who was unfaithful, or by a secret that was publicly revealed. But few of us have ever suffered anything close to what Jesus experienced.

They disrespected the Son of God. They called him a liar and a lawbreaker. They spit on him, blindfolded him, laughed at him, called him names, played games with him, stripped him naked, dressed him up like a clown, and mocked him as if he were a fake king. These are the techniques of brainwashing. They are the tactics of evil people out of control.

What is the worst embarrassment you have ever experienced? What is the greatest humiliation you can imagine? Multiply that by a thousand. Feel the shame. Try to imagine the humiliation for the very good Jesus being treated so very badly. Try to feel just what it was like.

Without in any way minimizing the horror of that humiliation, it seems to me that his suffering from rejection was actually worse. I recently watched a film biography of Sir Winston Churchill. As prime minister of Great Britain during World War II, he was probably the greatest political leader of his generation. But did you know that after the war was over, after Germany was defeated and Britain was again safe, that Winston Churchill was rejected and lost the election as Prime Minister? What does it feel like to give your absolute best for the people you love and then have them turn against you?

That's what happened to Jesus. He had come as the Son of God on a mission of love. He didn't have to do it. He gave his very best. The Lord of heaven became a servant to help the poor, to heal the sick, to teach the truth. He was kind and good and loving. The best of the best!

And he was rejected. The Pharisees were a religious denomination that rejected Jesus because he healed sick people on the holy day. The Sadducees were a different religious denomination that rejected Jesus because he believed in the supernatural and life-after-death. One political party rejected him because he didn't support the government. Another political party rejected him because he didn't oppose the government. His treasurer and CFO (Judas) sold him out for a cash bribe. His close friend Peter denied knowing him out of fear that he would be named in a government indictment.

It hurts to be rejected. We all want to be liked. We all want to be accepted. We all want to be understood and appreciated. To be abandoned and rejected by just about everyone plays a game on our emotions. It is painful to the point of suffering. Even if it is deserved, it is painful. When it is undeserved, it is double suffering.

When Jesus was humiliated, tried, rejected by just about everyone, scourged, and crucified, it did a job on his head. He felt desperately alone. There is a pain to loneliness and isolation that tortures the soul.

Jesus just took it. He didn't say much to reveal his heart—until he was almost dead. He said something I don't pretend to fully understand in Mark 15:34: *"And at three in the afternoon, Jesus cried out in a loud voice, 'Eloi, Eloi, lema sabachthani?' (which means, 'My God, my God, why have you forsaken me?')."*

It was three o'clock in the afternoon, and Jesus was dying. The rejection had built up to the point where he concluded that even God had forsaken him.

I have thought about what this line means more than maybe any other line in the New Testament. I do not think that God the Father had forsaken or abandoned Jesus at the peak of his pain, but I think that Jesus thought God had rejected him just like everyone else. That's what we all do. When everyone is turning against us, we assume that God is in the same camp. When everything has gone terribly wrong, we think that God the Father has forsaken us, too. For Jesus it was an unspeakable horror to have that level of loneliness. It was the apex of suffering, the depth of his fear. He was facing the worst experience in the history of the universe, and he felt he had to do it absolutely alone, that he was abandoned even by God.

When we feel alone and rejected, we understand some of what Jesus suffered. Some days we may feel what he felt—forsaken by God. As real as those feelings may be, the truth is that God is there whether we feel his presence or not. The truth for us is that Jesus is with us even when we accuse him of forsaking us. He is there, and he fully understands.

But there is one way that Jesus suffered that we cannot understand. It was actually the epicenter of his suffering. It was what his suffering was all about. It was when human sin was placed on the Son of God. It is described in the New Testament in such places as 1 Peter 2:24: *" '[Jesus] himself bore our sins' in his body on the cross, so that we might die to sins and live for righteousness; 'by his wounds you have been healed.' "* Or, 2 Corinthians 5:21, *"God made him who had no sin to be sin for us, so that in him we might become the righteousness of God."*

At an unspecified point on that Friday when Jesus was being crucified, God gave our sin to Jesus. It was as if we were there. Amazingly, the Bible never explains to us how God did this. It is too profound, too mysterious, and too supernatural for us to understand. But we can benefit from the result even if we cannot comprehend the process.

There is, however, a hint of what happened. It is captured in words Jesus prayed in the Garden of Gethsemane on the eve of his crucifixion. When three times he prayed on the eve of his crucifixion and asked for a way out, he referred to the coming "cup." In Matthew 26:39 we are told that he "fell with his face to the ground and prayed, *'My Father, if it is possible, may this cup be taken from me.'* " The "cup" of his suffering included all that was coming, but specifically it meant the experience of human sin.

Think of it like this. Imagine the worst concoction of toxic waste—a cesspool of every communicable disease from bubonic plague to HIV to the Ebola virus; human waste sampled from every major sewage treatment plant and septic tank in the world; environmental waste from chemical factories in America to nuclear waste from Chernobyl in the former Soviet Union.

Imagine it all put together—the foulest smells, the strongest diseases—and then imagine that somehow it was concentrated down to the contents of a single cup of poison so deadly that its fumes burn the lining of your lungs and a single drop sears holes in your esophagus. It is a totally disgusting, repulsive, and deadly concoction. Drink it, and you are dead.

Now compare that to the "cup" of Jesus. The cup of Jesus was filled with human sin. Not bacteria, viruses, sewage, and pollution. But this cup was filled with idolatry, incest, adultery, abuse, lying, lust, stealing, selfishness, and every other variety of sin. Flavoring this cup were the most heinous violent crimes that stream across our headlines and the most subtle secret sins that are hidden in the thoughts of outwardly noble people. This cup concentrated all human evil. Everything each of us has ever done and will do that is displeasing to God was in that cup. Every one of us made our contribution to the cup. In its most diluted form, it was a deadly drink. In its dense concentration, it was evil in a mug.

It is no wonder Jesus prayed, *"My Father . . . may this cup be taken from me."* The sight and smell of it made him deathly ill. He knew that to actually drink it would be terror; it would be suffering beyond imagination. 2 Corinthians 5:21 says, *"God made him who had no sin to be sin for us."*

And then he suffered death. We think that it was the cross that killed him. It was really the sin. Understand that crucifixion usually took days. Jesus was crucified around noon and he was dead by 3 PM. That was a very quick death for crucifixion. Often those who were crucified suffered for days and died from exposure and thirst.

We dare not minimize the physical suffering of the cross. To be sure, it was horrendous. Romans saw capital punishment very differently from the way present-day Americans view it. The Constitution of the United States forbids cruel and unusual punishment. In fact, many consider capital punishment itself to be cruel and unusual. But those who advocate capital punishment insist that it should be as humane as possible. Whether it is the noose or the guillotine, a firing squad or the electric chair, the practice has been for a quick death with minimal suffering. Hoods are placed on the heads of those who are executed. Strict limits are placed on who can witness the death.

The Romans didn't see it that way at all. They wanted executions to be painful, public, and protracted. They wanted victims to suffer long. They wanted everyone to see. They wanted victims to be humiliated. They made it as bad as they could. To be nailed to a cross was not primarily capital punishment that happened to hurt. It was lengthy torture that happened to kill. Jesus suffered as awful an execution as perverted human imagination could dream up.

Finally the end came. Mark 15:37 tells us, *"With a loud cry, Jesus breathed his last."* At last it was over. The suffering was done. Jesus had successfully completed his mission. The pain and punishment for human sin was paid in full. Not one more man or woman, boy or girl need ever again be alienated from God. Hell need never be anyone's destiny.

There is an old Christian hymn called "When I Survey the Wondrous Cross." It puts the suffering of Jesus into personal perspective when it concludes by saying, "Love so amazing, so divine, demands my soul, my life, my all."

Simply put, the suffering of Jesus on behalf of others demands a response. After all, it was for us that he suffered. He loved us. He died for us. He did his part and invites us to accept his suffering and sacrifice. Call it faith. Call it belief. Call it accepting Jesus as personal Savior. However we describe our response, it is telling God that we say good-bye to our sins and trust Jesus for our eternal destiny.

I want us to be sure we all know exactly how to respond. I invite you to personalize your response to what Jesus has done. Pray a prayer of faith in which you tell God that you accept what Jesus did. Your prayer might go something like this:

Jesus, I thank you for suffering and dying for me. Thank you for taking the punishment for my sin. I believe in you. I accept what you did. I give you my life in gratitude for what you did for me. Please, be my Savior from sin and the Lord of my life forever. Amen.

Worship Through Giving

"How Deep the Father's Love for Us" by Stuart Townsend (© 1995 Thankyou Music (Admin. by EMI Christian Music Publishing))

Key Lyrics: How deep the Father's love for us, how vast beyond all measure that he should give his only Son to make a wretch his treasure. How great the pain of searing loss, the Father turns his face away as wounds which mar the Chosen One bring many to glory"

Resource: Listening CD—*The Wonderful Cross: Modern Worship Songs Celebrating the Cross* (available at www.worshiptogether.com). Printed music at www.songdiscovery.com.

Video Idea: Use a variety of video clips from the films about Jesus and feature clips based upon his suffering and ultimate crucifixion. Have the video run during the song to provide a visual level of meaning.

Worship Through Music

"Hallelujah What a Savior" words and music by Philip Bliss (Public domain), arr. Kauflin (© 1998 Sovereign Grace Praise (BMI))

Key Lyrics: "'Man of Sorrows' what a name, for the Son of God who came, ruined sinners to reclaim, Hallelujah what a Savior"

Resource: Listening CD—*Upward: The Bob Kauflin Hymns Project.* Both the CD and printed music are available at www.sovereigngrace ministries.org/music/projects/hymns/upward.html.

This classic hymn was re-harmonized and arranged in a contemporary setting by Bob Kauflin. It is a stirring and almost haunting hymn ballad reminding us of the suffering and sacrifice of Jesus Christ on our behalf.

"The Wonderful Cross" original words by Isaac Watts, original music by Lowell Mason (Public domain) additional refrain by Chris Tomlin, J.D. Walt, and Jesse Reeves (© 2000 Worshiptogether.com/Six Steps Publishing)

Key Lyrics: "my richest gain I count but loss and pour contempt on all my pride"

Video Option: At the end of the song, show an image of a cross on screens while the band plays an extended instrumental ending. If you have the capabilities, a moving flash image of a cross would add a special dynamic as people reflect on the message of the cross of Jesus Christ as a symbol of perfect humility.

Resource: Listening CD—*Song Discovery Volume 25.* Listening CD—*The Noise We Make,* by Chris Tomlin (available at www.grassrootsmusic.com). Printed music at www.songdiscovery.com.

This is the classic hymn "When I Survey the Wondrous Cross" adapted for contemporary settings with a new chorus added that adds the challenge, "O the wonderful cross bids me come and die and find that I may truly live." It is a direct tie to the sermon.

FaithStory

Many people come to Jesus Christ because their personal suffering has driven them to do so. The faith story for this week should feature such a personal experience. Your challenge will be to help the presenter speak in such a way that the content of their suffering does not diminish our focus on Jesus Christ.

Worship Through Music

"Blessed Be Your Name" by Matt Redman (© 2002 Thankyou Music)

Key Lyrics: "Blessed be your name in the land that is plentiful, where your streams of abundance flow…blessed be your name. And blessed be your name when I'm found in the desert place, though I walk through the wilderness, blessed be your name"

Resource: Listening CD—*Blessed Be Your Name: The Songs of Matt Redman*, vol 1., by Matt Redman (Sparrow, 2005). Printed music at www.praisecharts.com.

Benediction

Remember the suffering of Jesus, and be blessed by all he has done for you. Amen.

TRADITIONAL WORSHIP MUSIC OPTIONS:

Call to Worship Choir Anthem

"Hosanna in the Highest" by Craig Courtney (© 2002 Beckenhorst Press)

Key Lyrics: "Holy, holy, holy Lord, God of power and might, heav'n and earth are full of your glory…Hosanna, hosanna, hosanna in the highest"

Palm Sunday Responsive Reading

Psalm 24:7–10
Leader:
Lift up your heads, you gates;

All:
Be lifted up, you ancient doors,
That the King of glory may come in

Leader:
Who is this King of glory?

All:
The LORD strong and mighty
The LORD mighty in battle

Leader:
Lift up your heads, you gates;

All:
Lift them up, you ancient doors,
That the King of glory may come in.

Leader:
Who is he, this King of glory?

All:
The LORD Almighty—
He is the King of glory.

Hymn Options

"All Glory Laud and Honor" words by Theodulph of Orleans, tr. John Mason Neale, music by Melchoir Teschner; harm. by W.H. Monk; desc. Hustad (Public domain)

Key Lyrics: "All glory, laud and honor to thee, Redeemer, King...to whom the lips of children made sweet hosannas ring."

"Hosanna Loud Hosanna" words by Jeanette Threlfall, music by Hofkapelle, adapt. and harm. by W.H. Monk (Public domain)

Key Lyrics: "Hosanna, loud hosanna the little children sang through pillared court and temple the lovely anthem rang"

"Ride On Ride On in Majesty" words by Henry H. Milman, music by Lowell Mason (Public domain)

Key Lyrics: "Ride on, ride on in majesty your last and fiercest strife is nigh...the Father on his sapphire throne awaits his own anointed Son"

"Lift High the Cross" words by George William Kitchin, and Michael Robert Newbolt, music by Sydney Hugo Nicholson (© 1974 Hope Publishing Company)

Key Lyrics: "Lift high the cross, the love of Christ proclaim till all the world adore his sacred name"

"In the Cross of Christ I Glory" words by John Bowring, music by Ithamar Conkey (Public domain)

Key Lyrics: "In the cross of Christ I glory there for all was grace made free…None deserving, yet receiving life thro' death at Calvary"

Service 7

Easter: Seeing For Yourself

THEME

Easter

BIBLE PASSAGES

Luke 24

SUMMARY

Easter was scary and exciting. There were supernatural creatures and spectacular miracles. Some believed that Jesus was still dead even though the tomb was empty. Some believed just because they were told what happened. Some ran to see for themselves. Some walked and talked with Jesus and still couldn't see what happened.

SERVICE IMAGE

The DVD features a graphic image suitable for use during the "Easter: Seeing For Yourself" service. This suggested worship background shows pink tulips against a green backdrop. This worship background appears on the *Abingdon Worship Photos, vol 3: Projection Images for Lent and Easter,* by Jim and Mary Whitmer (2003, Abingdon).

BLENDED SERVICE SEQUENCE:

Prelude

Traditional Option (Organ Solo)

"Christ Lay In Death's Dark Bonds" by Bach (Public domain)

Contemporary Option

"Worthy Is the Lamb Medley" Words and Music by Darlene Zschech, Fanny J. Crosby, Mathew Bridges, George J. Elvey arranged by Dan Galbraith (© Integrity's Hosanna Music)

Key Lyrics: "Thank you for the Cross Lord, thank you for the price you paid . . . bearing all my sin and shame in love you came"

Resources: This medley was recorded on the CD Unashamed Love by Integrity Music. The CD and a DVD video sync (iWORSHIP, volume G, song 4) is available through www.integritymusic.com. Printed music is available at www.praisecharts.com.

Invocation

Worship Through Music and Drama

"Christ the Lord Is Risen Today" words by Charles Wesley (Public domain)

Key Lyrics: "Christ the Lord is risen today, Alleluia . . . all creation, join to say Alleluia . . . raise your joys and triumphs high, Alleluia. Sing, ye heavens, and earth reply, Alleluia"

"Rejoice, the Lord is King" words by Charles Wesley, music by John Darwall (Public domain)

Key Lyrics: "Rejoice, the Lord is King, your Lord and King adore. Rejoice, give thanks, and sing and triumph evermore"

Dramatic Bible Reading (With soft music underscore)

Characters: NARRATOR—contemporary clothes (or back stage)
THOMAS—biblical clothes
JESUS—contemporary clothes with a white robe over top
MARY MAGDALENE (no lines)—biblical clothes

NARRATOR *(Mark 16:9–13; John 20:24–26):* When Jesus rose early on the first day of the week, he appeared first to Mary Magdalene . . . She went and told those who had been with him and who were mourning and weeping. When they heard that Jesus was alive and that she had seen him, they did not believe it. Afterward Jesus appeared in a different form to two of them while they were walking in the country. These returned and reported it to the rest; but they did not believe them either. Now Thomas (also known as Didymus), one of the Twelve, was not with the disciples when Jesus came. So the other disciples told him, "We have seen the Lord!" But he said to them,

THOMAS: "Unless I see the nail marks in his hands and put my finger where the nails were, and put my hand into his side, I will not believe."

NARRATOR: A week later his disciples were in the house again, and Thomas was with them. Though the doors were locked, Jesus came and stood among them and said,

JESUS *(John 20:26b–27):* "Peace be with you!" "Put your finger here; see my hands. Reach out your hand and put it into my side. Stop doubting and believe."

THOMAS *(John 20:28):* "My Lord and my God!"

JESUS *(John 20:29):* "Because you have seen me, you have believed; blessed are those who have not seen and yet have believed."

[Jesus removes white robe to reveal contemporary clothing, faces the audience and says line again]

JESUS *(John 20:29): [Motioning to the audience]* Blessed are those who have not seen me and yet have believed."

"My Redeemer Lives" by Reuben Morgan (© 1998 Reuben Morgan/ Hillsongs Australia, ASCAP)

Key Lyrics: "I'll raise a banner . . . 'Cause my Lord has conquered the grave . . . My Redeemer lives"

Resource: Listening CD—*World Through Your Eyes,* by Reuben Morgan (2005, Rocketown). Listening CD—*Extravagant Worship: The Songs of Reuben Morgan* (Hillsong).

"Christ the Lord Is Risen Today" (Reprise) words by Charles Wesley (Public domain)

Key Lyrics: Final verse: "Soar we now where Christ has led, Alleluia! Following our exalted Head, Alleluia! Made like him, like him we rise, Alleluia! Ours the cross, the grave, the skies. Alleluia!"

Welcome

FaithStory

Ideally, the faith story would be a person that came to Christ through an Easter experience. Or, perhaps someone that previously participated in the life of the church only on Christmas and Easter, but now has found a deeper relationship with Christ and the community of faith to be a daily desire.

Worship Through Giving

Choir Anthem

"Hallelujah from Christ on the Mount of Olives" by Beethoven (Public domain)

Key Lyrics: "Hallelujah unto God's Almighty Son"

Worship Through Teaching

SEEING FOR YOURSELF
Luke 24

The JESUS film presents the life of Jesus Christ as recorded in the New Testament Gospel of Luke. It has been translated into 871 different languages and has been seen by almost six billion people around the globe. For many of those people, it is the first time they have ever seen or heard anything about Jesus Christ. For one audience in an East Asian jungle, it was not only the first time they heard the story of Jesus, but it was the first time they had ever seen a movie!

Outside, after dark, the projector started up, and the motion picture appeared on the screen. The crowd was attracted to the Jesus who performed miracles, healed the sick, and loved little children. But when this good man was arrested and beaten by soldiers, the crowd was outraged. They demanded that this cruelty be stopped.

When the cruelty continued, they attacked the missionary who was operating the projector, assuming that somehow he was responsible for this cruelty and injustice. He had no choice but to stop the projector and explain that it wasn't over yet; there was more to come. So, the crowd settled down, and the film began again.

But when the film came to the crucifixion, they lost control. People wept and wailed. The sounds were so loud that the film again had to be stopped until the audience calmed down. Again they were told that the story wasn't over; there was more to see.

When they were quiet enough to start again, the film came back on, and they watched the Resurrection. Pandemonium broke out. A party started. There was singing and dancing, shouting and slapping each other on the back in celebration. The cheers and shouts of joy were deafening.

The missionary once again stopped the projector, but he didn't tell them to calm down. They were doing exactly what should be done when experiencing the Resurrection of Jesus. Shout and jump and dance and celebrate!

The story they saw on film is the same one we read in the New Testament book of Luke. Luke 24:1–8 begins with a group of women who came to grieve over Jesus's dead body:

On the first day of the week, very early in the morning, the women took the spices they had prepared and went to the tomb. They found the stone rolled away from the tomb, but when they entered, they did not find the body of the Lord Jesus. While they were wondering about this, suddenly two men in clothes that gleamed like lightening stood beside them. In their fright the women bowed down with their faces to the ground, but the men said to them, "Why do you look for the living among the dead? He is not here; he has risen! Remember how he told you, while he was still with you in Galilee: 'The Son of Man must be delivered over into the hands of sinners, be crucified and on the third day be raised again.'" Then they remembered his words.

Up until that moment, they had given up all hope. Desperation had set in. Dead was dead, and they might as well accept it because it was something they could not change. These friends and family of Jesus didn't come with faith or high expectations. They came with grief, sadness, and defeat. When they saw that Jesus's body was missing, it never occurred to them that anything supernatural had happened. They didn't know what had happened.

Two very bright angels appeared to the women and just about scared them to death. Filled with fear, they fell to the ground and put their faces in the dirt because they were so frightened. Then they heard these angels announce that Jesus was alive again. He had risen from the dead.

That seemed highly unlikely. It sounded impossible until they remembered that Jesus had actually predicted that this would happen. They had seen his miracles. They had heard his teaching. They knew his character. What Jesus had predicted had come true.

For women and men of every generation this is what Jesus does. He brings hope to replace grief; he brings new life right out of death. For those who feel hopeless, the Easter resurrection of Jesus is the very best news we could ever hear.

These women had to tell! They rushed into the city of Jerusalem to report to Jesus's other disciples who were hiding out in a safe house. In Luke 24:9–12 we are told:

When they came back from the tomb, they told all these things to the Eleven and to all the others. It was Mary Magdalene, Joanna, Mary the mother of James, and the others with them who told this to the apostles. But they did not believe the women, because their words seemed to them like nonsense. Peter, however, got up and ran to the tomb. Bending over, he saw the strips of linen lying by themselves, and he went away, wondering to himself what had happened.

Have you ever told the truth and no one would believe you? You were all excited but no one seemed to care? Jesus's coming back to life seemed too farfetched for any of them to believe. It sounded to them like absolute nonsense. But Peter wondered, "What if it really happened?" Maybe it was true! So, on the outside chance, he ran to the tomb to see for himself.

Peter is like all of us who are naturally skeptical. The difference is that he was willing to check out the possibility, even if he had his doubts. He went to the tomb and found it empty. It wasn't absolute proof, but it was enough to start him down the road to faith.

Luke 24:13–32 tells about a couple who one night were walking the seven miles from Jerusalem to their hometown of Emmaus. While they were walking, a stranger came along and walked and talked with them. He asked what they were talking about. They were surprised to hear that he didn't know the big news. In verses 18–24 we hear the following dialogue:

> *One of them, named Cleopas, asked him, "Are you only a visitor to Jerusalem and do not know the things that have happened there in these days?" "What things?" [the stranger] asked. "About Jesus of Nazareth," they replied. "He was a prophet, powerful in word and deed before God and all the people. The chief priests and our rulers handed him over to be sentenced to death, and they crucified him; but we had hoped that he was the one who was going to redeem Israel. And what is more, it is the third day since all this took place. In addition, some of our women amazed us. They went to the tomb early this morning but didn't find his body. They came and told us that they had seen a vision of angels, who said he was alive. Then some of our companions went to the tomb and found it just as the women had said, but him they did not see."*

Then this stranger started to talk about how the news perfectly fit with all the prophecies in the Old Testament. The couple was dazzled by the information and insights of the stranger so they invited him home for dinner. During dinner, they suddenly realized this was no stranger. This was Jesus! It was true! He was alive—and right there eating dinner and talking with them.

How could it take them so long to recognize and believe when Jesus was right there in front of them? Well, there have been lots of people like Cleopas. There are all kinds of stories of those who have been close to Jesus and never recognized who he was. That's what the Easter story is all about. It's about opening our eyes so that we can see the truth about Jesus for ourselves—truth that was there all along.

This couple from Emmaus was so thrilled that they practically ran the seven miles back to Jerusalem to report what had happened. They searched out the group of Jesus's family and friends who were hiding in that house, and they burst in and announced, "It is true! The Lord has risen!"

Everyone was talking at once. There was a hubbub of conversation, stories, reports, questions and excitement. Then, according to Luke 24:36, "*While they were still talking about this, Jesus himself stood among them and said to them, 'Peace be with you.'*"

Suddenly everyone was silent. They were startled, shocked, and scared. They thought he was a ghost! But he was no ghost. Jesus was alive, and Jesus was there. Jesus told them, *"Look at my hands and my feet. It is I myself! Touch me and see; a ghost does not have flesh and bones, as you see I have."*

That was just like Jesus. He stepped right into their lives and homes to show himself up-close and personal. When they saw his scars, they jumped for joy and amazement. It was like that showing of the movie in the jungle when pandemonium broke out!

This Easter, you are invited to come and see Jesus for yourself. See Jesus on the movie screen. See Jesus in the Bible. See Jesus in the Easter story. See Jesus in your prayers. See Jesus in your dreams. See Jesus in your home. See Jesus in the strangers God sends you. See Jesus in the circumstances of your life. See Jesus. Experience Jesus. Believe Jesus. Accept Jesus as Savior and Lord. He will transform your life from here all the way to eternity.

Following the 1917 Bolshevik Revolution, the dictator Josef Stalin wanted to eradicate Christianity from across Russia and replace it with Communist atheism. He sent teachers, touring commissars, who went to every city and town and village, even the most remote places in the Soviet Union, to give lectures denouncing Jesus Christ and replacing him with Karl Marx.

After one such speech to an assembly of peasants in a rural village, the commissar had talked a very long time and was convinced that he had talked them out of their faith and into his atheism. When he sat down, the assembly hall was silent. But then a Russian Orthodox priest stood in the back of the assembly hall and shouted out, "I have one thing to say to you: Christ is risen!" And the entire crowd immediately and resoundingly responded, "Christ is risen, indeed!"

They had seen him for themselves. They had experienced him in their lives. They believed—and nothing, nothing was going to dissuade them.

This Easter, see Jesus for yourself. Experience the risen Christ. Believe in him and be transformed from now to eternity.

Prayer: *God of the cross and God of Easter: How we thank you for the truth of your Son, Jesus Christ. But we want to say it one more time: as much as we believe all that the Bible says, it is not enough! We want to experience Jesus for ourselves. Let us see him. Let us know him. Let us be transformed by him. Let us say: "Christ is risen! He is risen, indeed." Amen.*

Worship Through Giving

"End of the Beginning" by David Phelps (© 2001 Winkin' Music/Soulwriter Music Company, Inc.)

Key Lyrics: "His death wasn't the end but the beginning of life that's completed in you . . .

Resource: Listening CD—*David Phelps,* by David Phelps (2002 Spring Hill [Wea 406]).

Worship Through Music

"Crown Him with Many Crowns" words by Matthew Bridges and Godfrey Thring, music by George J. Elvey (Public domain)

Key Lyrics: "Awake, my soul, and sing of him who died for thee and hail him as thy matchless king through all eternity"

Benediction

Pastor: See for yourself. Jesus Christ has risen!

People: He has risen indeed!

Pastor: Amen.

Appendix
Using the DVD

Playing the DVD on a Set-top Player

Set-top DVD players are connected to a TV. If you have previously played a DVD motion picture, you will see that the *Igniting Worship Series: 40 Days with Jesus* DVD behaves in much the same way. Once inserted, the disk will begin playing automatically, beginning with the copyright notice and logos. After these have played, the **Main Menu** will appear, and you may then choose what you would like to view.

To navigate through the DVD menus, use the **Up** and **Down** arrow keys on your remote to move the pointer to the menu item that you wish to play. After an item is highlighted, press **Play** or **Enter** to move to the next screen or to begin playing an item such as a video. Clicking on the **Title** button will take you back to the very beginning of the disk.

Volume is also adjusted in the normal way for your DVD player. Other buttons on the remote, like **Fast Forward**, will allow you to quickly move through a video.

All of the screens also have embedded graphical buttons, such as **Menu**, to help you navigate. Selecting the graphical **Menu** button will take you back one level in the menu structure, depending on where you are. Selecting the **Back** or **Next** button will move you through the other menus at the same level.

Playing the DVD on a Computer

System Requirements

Windows
- Windows 98 and higher (ME or higher recommended)
- At least 600 MHz processor (1Ghz or higher recommended)
- 128 MB of memory (256 recommended)
- DVD-ROM drive with appropriate drivers and software

Macintosh
- OS 9 or higher
- G3 processor (600 Mhz or higher)
- At least 128 MB of memory (256 recommended)
- DVD-ROM drive with appropriate drivers and software

If you have the capability to hook a computer with a DVD player to a projector, you may choose to use this method to display the video components for the services. Every computer will have a different type of proprietary software that comes with the DVD-ROM drive, and the controls on each will vary slightly.

Many of the buttons on the software interface will act just like the buttons on a DVD remote, though there will be some variation. Using the **Up** and **Down** arrow buttons on your software remote will cycle through and highlight each of the buttons, functioning just as they do on a set-top DVD player. (**Up** and **Left** will move through the buttons clockwise; **Down** and **Right** will move through the buttons counter-clockwise.) Once you have highlighted the button you want, hit the **Enter** key to activate the button. The advantage, however, of the computer navigation over the DVD set-top player is your ability to use the mouse to easily select the item you want by clicking it.

In general, clicking the **Menu** button will take you back one step: if you are simply in a menu, it will take you up one level to the previous one; if you are playing a video, it will stop the video and take you back to the sub-menu. You can also use the **Menu** button to exit out of a video and return to the menu. Depending on where you are, you may have several choices when you click the **Menu** button. **Title** takes you back to the very beginning of the disk. **Root** takes you back to the previous menu (if this is your only other choice). The **Fast Forward** and **Rewind** buttons will allow you to advance or rewind the video.

Additional Resources on the DVD

How Do I Access these Resources?

To access the resources included on the DVD, you will need to place it in a computer DVD-ROM drive. To browse to these data folders in Windows, open **Windows Explorer** and find the **Igniting Worship** disk icon. Double-click the DVD icon for a listing of the contents. (Be patient; it may take several seconds for this list to appear.) You may also use My Computer to get a listing of the data folders. However, you will probably need to right-click the DVD icon and choose Explore rather than double-click the DVD icon since this might cause the DVD to begin playing. On a Macintosh, simply double-click the DVD icon to view the contents of the disk.

Look in the "**Additional Resources**" folder to locate the file you need. Once you have located the file, either copy it to your hard drive or double-click the file to open it from the disk. If you open the file from the disk, remember that manipulating the file this way may be slower than copying it to your hard drive.

Below you will find detailed descriptions of the various types of resources available on the DVD and suggestions for how to use them.

Video

Videos are on the DVD in the folder "**Additional Resources**," and they are available in two MPEG sizes, 320x240 and 640x480. These clips have been included as MPEG-1 (.mpg) files. The MPEG-1 files are highly compressed and can be easily manipulated and inserted into Microsoft® PowerPoint® or other presentation package software. MPEG-1 can be viewed in most media players such as Windows® Media Player, Real® Player, and Apple QuickTime® Player.

Finished Video

The DVD includes the non-commercial videos that are described in the text. The videos have music beds, which may be played or turned down to allow your musicians to play. Transitions, music beds, and text have been added to create a finished presentation lasting several minutes. These clips may be used as a complete whole. The videos are: Temptation, Friends, Praying, and Resurrection.

Permissions

You may use these video clips only in the context of a worship service, provided you include the following acknowledgement in your presentation:

Video clip from *Igniting Worship: 40 Days with Jesus*, by Leith Anderson, Dan Collison, and SpiritFilms™ © 2006 Abingdon Press. Used by permission.

Dramas

Dramas are on the DVD in the folder "**Additional Resources**," and they are available in two MPEG sizes, 320x240 and 640x480. These clips have been included as MPEG-1 (.mpg) files. The MPEG-1 files are highly compressed and can be easily manipulated and inserted into Microsoft® PowerPoint® or other presentation software. MPEG-1 can be viewed in most media players such as Windows® Media Player, Real® Player, and Apple QuickTime® Player.

Drama scripts are on the DVD in the folder "**Additional Resources**." These scripts are available as Word documents.

Worship Backgrounds

There are separate worship backgrounds designed to compliment each service theme, including those for which no video is provided. Each set contains three graphic images, in both BMP and JPEG formats. Image samples can be viewed through the DVD interface.

Main

The main image contains the service title and can be displayed throughout your worship experience to fill any visual "holes" that would normally be a blank screen. This main image can also be used to provide smooth transitions between elements of the service.

No Words

This is the main image without the service title. You can use this image and add your own custom sermon points or additional illustrations. This design is best for smaller amounts of text. (If you have more than just a few lines of text, use the song background.)

Song Lyric

On the song background, a portion of the main image has been blurred so that text placed over it can easily be read. This background is useful for song lyrics, Scriptures, responsive prayers, and anything else containing more than a couple of lines of text.